The Pedagogy of Creativity

Anna Herbert

Routledge
Taylor & Francis Group

LONDON AND NEW YORK

This first edition published 2010
by Routledge
2 Park Square, Milton Park, Abingdon, Oxon OX14 4RN

Simultaneously published in the USA and Canada
by Routledge
270 Madison Ave, New York, NY 10016

Routledge is an imprint of the Taylor & Francis Group, an informa business

© 2010 Anna Herbert

Typeset in Sabon by Wearset Ltd, Boldon, Tyne and Wear
Printed and bound in Great Britain by TJ International Ltd,
Padstow, Cornwall

British Library Cataloguing in Publication Data
A catalogue record for this book is available from the British
Library

Library of Congress Cataloging-in-Publication Data
Herbert, Anna-Karin.
The pedagogy of creativity/Anna-Karin Herbert.
p. cm.
1. Creative teaching–Philosophy. 2. Creative ability–Psychological
aspects. 3. Educational psychology. I. Title.
LB1027.H3985 2010
370.15'7–dc22

2009037631

ISBN10: 0-415-54886-1 (hbk)
ISBN10: 0-415-54887-X (pbk)
ISBN10: 0-203-85546-9 (ebk)

ISBN13: 978-0-415-54886-1 (hbk)
ISBN13: 978-0-415-54887-8 (pbk)
ISBN13: 978-0-203-85546-1 (ebk)

Contents

Acknowledgements

Quotes reproduced with thanks from:

- The Society of Authors as the Literary Representative of the Estate of Virginia Woolf.
- The Provost and Scholars of King's College, Cambridge and The Society of Authors as the Literary Representative of the Estate of E.M. Forster.
- Quotes from the work of Karen Blixen reproduced with kind permission from the Rungstedlund Foundation.

Introduction

Creativity is an area of interest within pedagogy and has been for many years. This book offers an insight into current pedagogic research concerning creativity, neuropsychology and poststructuralist theory (Lacanian). New models and theories of creativity, along with classroom applications (methodology), are also presented. Further, the book attempts to discover what poststructuralist models of knowledge and learning might bring to the field of pedagogy both in terms of theory and practice.

There is a long tradition of research inspired by Lacanian theory within psychology and the human sciences. Pedagogic research, however, has largely been dominated by Anglo-Saxon traditions involving pragmatists such as Dewey and Mead. Lacanian theory enables the development of new models in which language and its influence on conscious and unconscious processes central to learning take precedence. These are supported by current neuropsychological research concerning language and the brain.

Taking a classroom-based example of poststructuralist methodology as a starting point, an investigation is made into the relationship between creativity seen in dreams and creativity in the classroom. Dreams have fascinated people throughout history. Who creates the dream narrative? Who stages the story of the dream? Who casts the various characters? Is there any evidence that this source of creativity can be used in the classroom? What might a methodology that taps into this form of creativity look like? Could such a methodology have any support in current neuropsychological theories of memory and learning? To answer these questions the relationship between creative thought and knowledge is discussed.

Three different kinds of knowledge exist according to Lacanian theory. The first is *connaissance*, which has its origins in the child's first meeting with its mirror image, and is therefore imaginary. The second is *savoir*, which has its origins in the Oedipus Complex, when the child comes into the symbolic dimension and accepts the law against incest. The third is *savoir-faire* or know-how, knowledge which is not expressed symbolically but physically. *Connaissance* is knowledge of the ego, which is conscious, while *savoir* is knowledge of the subject, which is unconscious. *Savoir-faire* is knowledge of the body, which is also unconscious (it is often called *silent knowledge* and is seen in physical skills such as riding a bike, hitting a hole-in-one or knocking a nail into the wall with a hammer). *Connaissance*, *savoir* and *savoir-faire* are, amongst other things, related to implicit and explicit memory, which in turn is the foundation of explicit knowledge and so-called *quiet knowledge* discussed within pedagogy. To understand these different kinds of knowledge we must first discover something about conscious and unconscious thought and its relation to language, as this is central to Lacan's theory of knowledge and creativity. To do so, Freud's theory of conscious thought, language and perception is discussed, along with neuropsychological and cognitive theories presented by Damasio, Gärdenfors and Sperry, amongst others.

In discussing Freud's theory of dream interpretation and the Wolfman's dream (1905), current dream research such as Hartman's neurotransmitter model, Winson's electrophysiological model, Hobson's activation–synthesis theory (A–S model) and Solms' cortical theory is presented. The conclusion that creativity in dreams is best understood in relation to the narrative of dreams (or the 'story teller') is arrived at, and an investigation into the origins of the 'story teller' is carried out so as to better understand the narrative of the dream, as well as how this source of creativity might be used in the classroom. Plato's *Apology 22* is discussed along with the Descartian subject, allowing for a comparison between the latter and the Lacanian subject. Freud's and Schiller's thoughts concerning creativity are also discussed (as set out in the interpretation of dreams). The subject speaks when the ego is in doubt, indicating that riddles, mysteries and puzzles are central to a methodology that aims at eliciting creativity. Also important ingredients in Lacanian pedagogy are: double negation; free association; nonsensical statements; and humour. The relationship between creativity and the 'gaze' of the Other (teacher, art critic, buyer, etc.) is discussed in relation to the visual arts and gesture (expressed in painting and writing).

Lacan describes a variety of possible relationships between creativity and knowledge in the four discourses. These enable an understanding of why learning and creativity is fun and give an indication as to how the joy of learning and creativity might be maintained. The four discourses also present a variety of relationships between the agent and the other. Translated into an educational setting we might position the teacher in place of the agent and the student in the position of the other. The Master's discourse describes the conditions for excellence. What are the conditions for excellence made by some teachers, and the conditions for the production of excellence achieved by some students? Why do they at times coincide and at other times not? In the Master's discourse the students have knowledge and are required to prove this by producing documents and sitting exams. However, there is always something outside or beyond the institutional expectations – object *a*. Teachers/lecturers call this *excellence* (the object of desire). The University discourse is driven by the command to 'learn more', the Hysteric's discourse leads to a desire for knowledge reflected through the desire for the agent (the students produce knowledge to please their teacher), and the Analyst's discourse leads to a production of knowledge and creativity caused by the desire to understand what the teacher/lecturer knows and what the teacher/lecturer expects, etc.

According to Lacan, knowledge is a means to *jouissance* or pleasure. Therefore the four discourses describe not only a relationship between the teacher and the student, but also the relationship between desire, knowledge and *jouissance*.

Both Schleiemacher and Schiller claim that pedagogy is an art form, taking shape within teacher–student interaction, or rather within a space emerging from this interaction. There would seem to be little in common between the manic artist and the teacher, but when considering some lessons which emerge spontaneously, at times even chaotically (either because the teacher has decided to set his/her plan aside or because of some unforeseen event in the classroom), compared to those which progress slowly and meticulously according to carefully pre-produced schedule plans, there seems to be a case to be made. The teacher/lecturer may emerge content from the former (as may students) but with very little memory of what actually happened. Added to this, it is very difficult to describe or write down anything about the experience for future reference. Other similar teaching experiences (i.e. experiences that are difficult to set in words) can be prompted by unexpected events in the classroom, which seem to cause a shift in the collective understanding of the subject at hand, such as an odd question posed by a student, or a sudden noise from the neighbouring room. When the bell rings and the students emerge, blinking at the light, aware that something unusual has happened, there is a fundamental change, a crystallising experience, according to cognitive psychologists. Most of us have these experiences either as students or as teachers, but we don't have words or a discourse, even if the experience is profound. Lacanian theory enables us to look at these experiences, analyse them and set them into words. Here the interrelation between students and teachers is discussed in terms of the gaze and what it might do for the production of *savoir* and creativity during a lecture. Creativity is also discussed in terms of cognitive and neuropsychological theory – specifically then, creativity dependent on *savoir* (primary processes according to cognitive theory).

There are occasions when subject creativity seems to resist, revealing the insistence and sometimes even repetition of old cherished 'truths' in which the ego has invested heavily. Teachers (and students) can, for instance, become stuck in old arguments that are vented whenever the opportunity arises (seemingly unaware of the reiteration). Repetition can also involve repetitive dreams, neurotic symptoms, rituals and repetitive involuntary thought patterns such as negative thoughts. Repetition of destructive behavioural patterns can arise where individuals repeatedly sabotage their results by failing to hand in assignments on time or, alternatively, failing to finish exam papers that are well within their capability. However, repetition can also be pleasurable, such as shouting football anthems and slogans, or repeatedly listening to a favourite tune. Freud's and Lacan's theories concerning repetition are discussed here so as to investigate what these might bring to the classroom in terms of understanding the defence of old beliefs and outdated knowledge, as well as the other forms of repetition discussed previously.

Repeating old given truths would seem to indicate that the subject cannot forget or release information. Forgetting is as essential to learning as remembering! Luria describes the case of S, a man who cannot forget, along with the problems he encounters while attempting to block out unwanted memories that disturb him. Added to this, S also claimed that he had problems with metaphors. Research indicates that the use of metaphor is involved in both remembering and 'forgetting', and is also important for creativity.

The Other is important when considering the role creativity might play in finding solutions to problems that arise in the classroom, such as aggression, feelings of inadequacy and fear of the unknown. A meeting with the Other can become a source of creativity in and of itself, as long as the ego's narcissistic response does not get in the way. This response is a problem in all educational situations and therefore deserves an investigation in its own right. Narcissism has its origins in the mirror stage, according to Lacan, when the child first greets its own image with competition and then with attraction), a response which is elicited in every relationship with other subjects (people). Further competitive jealousy and aggression is connected to sibling rivalry or times when other children are given more attention by the mOther. Feelings of inadequacy also hark back to the child's earliest development, when it understands that it cannot control the actions of the mOther as the child is too small and powerless. Feelings of inadequacy, competitive aggression and jealousy are therefore a natural part of pedagogic reality if we accept Lacanian developmental theory, and are therefore not 'alien' components to the classroom or a sign of impending failure. They do, however, need management. The right kind of methodology and good governance is a trusted classroom remedy, a remedy to which Lacanian theory also prescribes.

Relationships with the Other also involve an ethical dimension, according to Lacan, Levinas and Mead to mention a few (theories which will be discussed in this book). The Other is unknowable according to both Lacan and Levinas. It is 'beyond' – someone that can never be completely understood. For Levinas, the Other manifests itself as a face – and the face can only be changed by violence. Attempts to understand the incomprehensible by making the Other similar to someone previously known is committing violence against the other – metaphysical violence according to Levinas. Todd writes that, in response to the Other, we must develop a special kind of listening, a passive pre-verbal listening. The listener must avoid making meaning out of language. Disconnecting the ego's creation of meaning brings forth the subject (pre-verbal does not mean pre-symbolic). The subject then not only speaks, it listens. It listens, integrates and changes through the signifiers generated by the Other, expressed in signification. There is a creative listening, then, that belongs to the subject.

Learning from the Other is paradoxically also about learning in relation to ourselves. What is beyond in the Other also exists within us. The subject is beyond, and to a degree created by, the Other's signifiers. It is in alliance with the Other. Facing the unknowable Other is facing the unknowable dimensions in ourselves. This can be threatening to the ego and is often a cause of aggression. The ego does not like or accept its lack of mastery. However, Levinas' theory shows that: 'To be attentive is to recognize the mastery of the other, to react to his command.'

Visual arts, literature and media can be used as a means to elicit *savoir* and facilitate creative endeavour, as can music. I will discuss how these can help to develop creative methods. Further, I will discuss how free association can be used in conjunction with the above or used separately in exercises such as Jack Norin's creativity programme. I will also discuss the importance of student–teacher relations for the development of a creative organisational climate, along with other factors that facilitate the success of methods presented. Deconstruction (as presented by Derrida) enables a new perspective on old beliefs and knowledge. Deconstruction aims at the narrative or discourse maintaining these, and is therefore less likely to involve the ego's narcissism or mobilise defence mechanisms. This will also be discussed, along with lighter versions of discourse analysis.

Chapter 1

Towards a poststructuralist pedagogy

Introduction

When I was at university studying psychology, one lecturer inspired me more than any other and sent me down the path of teaching. That same lecturer became my PhD supervisor ten years later. Parveen Adams had an unwavering belief in the power of students' intellectual capacity (a characteristic of many great teachers), but this was perhaps not in and of itself as remarkable as the creativity she could unleash in a classroom – often shocking the unprepared students who had no idea of what might appear from the inner recesses of their minds during a classroom session. To add to the oddity of it, many students were at first reluctant to go to the classes, not because the content was uninteresting or the form was staid, but because of the complexity of the arguments produced, which were so far beyond us all that it left us feeling rather at a loss. However, we often felt we were in the presence of something great, witnessing the unfolding of a theory that might become world renowned and in which we might play a small part (Parveen was always generous in recognising any additions to her own work). In other words, however difficult the content, we did understand she was saying something important!

This frustrating situation initially caused anger. I had classmates who claimed they would never go to one of her lessons again after sitting dumbfounded throughout a 40-minute lecture of applied Lacanian theory. Then, after the third session, there seemed to be a slight ruffle underneath the surface of our struggling and bruised egos. Parveen would look up over her paper and ask a question about the film we had just seen (often a 50-year-old horror movie). Could we apply our theory? The classroom was silent and she would slowly wait for somebody brave enough to show their ignorance on the subject. The first tentative suggestion was often greeted with a nod or a smile, which led to a second attempt elsewhere in the classroom, and a third or a fourth, at which point somebody would say something quite outlandish out of pure exasperation, which would be followed by a deep silence. Not because of the outlandishness per se, but because it was the right form of outlandishness. The person (whoever it was) had managed to make an intelligent response without actually trying. There we have the first chapter of your PhD, Parveen would exclaim. And we all knew it to be true. This acted as a trigger – one strangely correct response after the next came, at first at a dribble and then a steady flow. We managed to make one amazing argument after the next and not a single one of us knew where it all came from other than that it was good work and our leader was standing in front of us like an orchestral conductor, whipping up a storm of creativity around her with seemingly no effort at all. After the session we would all feel strangely elated and simultaneously exhausted. We had been a part of something none of us had ever experienced before and most of us would probably never experience again. However, a small number of us tried to understand what had happened. For Parveen Adams had a technique, and while it might seem like magic, it was perfectly explicable and applicable to other situations of learning and creativity.

In the years that followed I was lucky to be one of Parveen's graduates and to study her methodology so as to form my own way of reproducing the creativity I experienced in the classroom to use in my own research. Like most graduates I caused my supervisor a great deal of consternation, refusing to follow exact guidance and insisting on finding my own rather unorthodox ways to develop theories (though I did not understand this until many years after my thesis was published). Parveen persevered and allowed me to make my own mistakes (of which I am very thankful). Now that I have been lecturing in my own college for some time and have had the opportunity to try out my supervisor's methodology with my own students (with varying results) I intend to put pen to paper and investigate the source of creativity inspired by Lacanian and Freudian theory. It is perhaps a rather daring project. I remember how I balked at doing anything with Lacan when Parveen first approached me with the possibility of working with Lacan's *Seminar VII*. I was writing a thesis on PTSD (post-traumatic stress disorder) and resisted as far as I possibly could, relenting only after having produced my MSc based on empirical studies and a qualitative application of Freudian theory.

What might Lacanian theory add to our understanding of the creative process?

Most creativity research is currently carried out by cognitive psychologists. They study creativity in relation to motivation, personality, IQ, cognitive processes, cultural factors, genetic factors, psychopathological factors, family patterns and neurological factors. Freud claimed the creative process was almost impossible to understand (when considering people like Dostoyevsky and other well-acclaimed creative geniuses) – it was either result of defence mechanisms, such as sublimation, or daydreaming.

The source of creativity described in Parveen's classroom would seem to be the unconscious (nobody could explain how or from where the creative answers emerged). In creativity research the involvement of primary (unconscious) processes is well established (even within cognitive research). These are considered to be part of a 'processing phase', after which an idea emerges (also described as the 'aha experience'). However, details as to how these primary processes function are very few and far between (other than suggesting that opposites are merged in a variety of ways that would not normally be possible, or that the right hemisphere is in some way involved).

Lacan offers a more detailed insight into the unconscious processes leading to creativity. Where cognitive models point to 'special' creative personalities, or the necessity of certain levels of IQ for creative endeavour, Lacan points to a creativity residing within, which is not dependent on motivation, genetic inheritance, personality, socio-economic background, position in the sibling group, anxiety levels, or the like. There are no differences between the creative (unconscious) mechanisms of people, only differences in the amount and quality of signifiers (which can always be adjusted simply by involving oneself in activities that provide a source for more signifiers).

Dreams have always been used as a source of inspiration for creative endeavour. Freud claimed that dreaming is a complicated 'intellectual' activity that involves organising the cohesive segments of dream scenarios into a 'story line' (not at all like psychotic episodes). This is supported by current research on dreams. Leading roles are cast, props are created, backdrops to the dream are put in place, much like in the various acts of a theatre play. We might ask how the processes described above (i.e. the story teller) relate to the creativity unleashed in Parveen's classroom – creative responses which at first seemed random but upon further inspection provided material for our thesis chapters (dealing with content which was far beyond the capacity of our conscious cognition at the time). Lacanian theory attempts to answer this question; addressing who or what is writing the play; what organising force causes us to play one or several major roles in a variety of scenarios, every night, several times a night for all of our lives (Freud focused on the message of the dream as opposed to the narrator).

Lacanian theory also enables an in-depth analysis of the importance of the 'Other' (as a person and as a source of language) in the creative process. We may, for instance, emerge from a lecture with the sense of something profound having happened (not necessarily connected to the conscious content of the lecture). We are no longer the same person who entered the lecture hall a few hours ago, we have been touched by the Other's message. A fundamental shift in perspective or understanding has occurred, causing a change, but few of us can explain what. At times whole audiences can be affected by this experience.

There are times when we emerge from having given a lecture or lesson without any memory of what actually happened (similar to arriving at work in the morning but not being able to remember any details about the journey). Time collapses – we are there for the students, lecturing 'out there with the Other', caught by the gaze of a hundred eyes, yet somehow unaware of the audience or ourselves. We become the message we are conveying. After these lectures, students emerge elated, claiming that the lecture was amazing, or that they learnt something they had never understood before, and we (often completely exhausted and drained of energy) wonder what precisely we have done, wishing there had been a camera somewhere recording this lost hour. Lacanian theory offers a discourse with which to explain and understand these creative experiences, including theories of the body as well as *savoir-faire* (bodily knowledge).

Concepts and obstacles

There is really only one obstacle to an investigation into the processes described above, and this is Lacan's language and use of concepts. Lacanian theory has often, and somewhat undeservedly, been given the reputation of being complex beyond the point of theoretical redemption, keeping a large part of the psychoanalytic community at bay with seemingly odd concepts, such as *object a*, borromean knots and the cloaking of psychic phenomena in mathematical formula. However, we must remember that these concepts, valuable as they may be to those who wish to maintain Lacan's esoteric reputation (and there are many), are simply an expression of the philosophical concerns of the time.

Lacan belonged to a large group of French philosophers and artists who happily borrowed concepts from each other and entertained each other with witty near-mysticisms in an environment of intense creativity. Sartre, Simonne de Beauvoir, Camus and Merleau-Ponty are just a few of the people Lacan used to socialise and compete with for fame and fortune. In attempting to clarify Lacanian terminology I studied several of these philosophers, as well as Kojève's reading of Hegel, which was very popular at the time (Lacan attended Kojève's seminars and these had great influence on his development of theory). I also read Saussure, Lévi-Strauss, Heidegger and Freud.

The reading of these philosophers is by no means necessary to understand Lacan, but ten years ago I was determined to not only understand him, but to chart him back through his own philosophical readings as far as I could go (even reading some Aristotle, Descartes and Kant), and this determination served me well in understanding what Lacan was attempting to do with his odd terms and theories and how I might apply this to my own research on PTSD. I remember when outlining my thesis proposal to one of the professors at my department, his reaction was incredulity at my choice of theory. He asked me, quite honestly, what Lacan had ever brought to the world in terms of an explanation of psychological phenomena. Having spent four years on showing precisely what Lacanian theory might bring to the understanding of PTSD, I have set my sights on clarifying Lacanian concepts and theory, much to the frustration of my thesis supervisor who, belonging to the group of highly creative philosophers using Lacanian theory understood by few and revered by many, wanted me to follow in her footsteps. Here, I am afraid, I have been a great disappointment. But maybe one day I might tire of attempting to make Lacan accessible outside of psychoanalytic circles and write a paper which gets accepted in Lacanian Ink. I do, however, respect and understand the importance of 'non-understanding' in relation to creativity and will explain later what I mean by this.

I have found that Lacanian theory offers much to those of us willing to work through the theoretical jargon, and so I will attempt to discover not only the sources of creativity in Lacanian theory, but also the usefulness of Lacanian theory to teachers who wish to understand important aspects of their classrooms. Is there, for instance, a desire for knowledge, and if so, how might we enhance it and maintain it (if indeed it does need maintaining)? Does Lacanian theory imply the makings of a socially or individually based pedagogy? How might the role of the teacher be understood in the light of this theory? What is knowledge, according to Lacan? How might a teacher use a Lacanian theory of knowledge in the classroom? What might Lacanian theory tell us about the tendency of repetition in the classroom (i.e. sticking to certain truths whether or not they are good for us – this applies to teachers and students alike)? How might Lacanian theory help us to understand aggression in the classroom? What importance might Lacanian pedagogy (if any) have for the intercultural dimensions of the classroom? How might we understand the relations of power in a classroom using Lacanian theory? I will also present some of Lacan's methodological devices for ensuring his readers' and listeners' unmitigated interest and creativity (i.e. those who did not turn away in frustration), as well as methods that I and other researchers in the field use in our daily work. But before we go on to look at the suggested areas described above, I will attempt to sketch out a theoretical background against which to understand Lacanian models and concepts, and in so doing, discuss and analyse Lacan's theory of knowledge (conscious and unconscious). This theory hinges on the concepts of the ego and the subject.

A comparison between Freud's and Lacan's theory of consciousness

Lacan became a member of the first psychoanalytic society in France under the direction of Marie Bonaparte shortly after he had obtained his doctorate in psychiatry. He has often been called 'the French

> The man who searches deeply for the truth, and wishes to avoid being deceived by false leads, must turn the light of his inner vision upon himself.
>
> (Boethius 2002 [523]: p. 61)

Freud', which is somewhat simplistic as his work borrows from many other thinkers. Lacan, however, did claim that his theories were based on a re-reading of Freudian theories, and therefore I will make an in-depth comparison between the two when discussing the subject, the ego and other central psychoanalytic concepts important to the investigation of the questions raised above. Both Lacan and Freud were physicians. In 1893 Freud discussed a group of patients suffering from motor paralysis which had no known neurological origin – the symptoms of paralysis were connected not to a real body, but to a constructed one. The paralysis of a hand, for instance, corresponded to a glove and not a physiological hand (i.e. represented a layperson's view of what a hand is). This led Freud to realise the importance of the signifier and signification in relation to the body, but also to become aware of the importance of the unconscious in terms of inhibiting the normal physiological functioning of limbs. On remembering the original cause of paralysis the disability disappeared, which in turn led Freud to develop a 'talking cure', which at first took the shape of free association.

Freud likened free association to the creative process discussed by Schiller in a letter to a friend suffering from writer's cramp. Schiller describes a flow that is enabled by circumventing self-critique. Freud later went on to discuss the source for this form of creativity in relation to dreams. Dreams, claimed Freud, were not chaotic – rather, they were lucid and followed a rationale, that of wish fulfilment, whether they be nightmares or otherwise. Freud concentrated on the message of the dream and how it could be interpreted. In a sleuth-like analysis he mercilessly investigated the clues held in his own dreams, laying out the logic of these, proceeding cautiously only when these became too sexual. Using the concepts of displacement and condensation in the description of the Wolfman's dreams somewhat later, he discussed how 'derivates' of repressed wishes disguised themselves (a fox becoming a wolf, for instance, in the Wolfman's dream) and slipped past the censor to the preconscious to emerge in the dream content. The dream was the royal road to the unconscious. This was about as much as could be said about the content of the unconscious as it was not accessible to conscious thought. All a therapist could do was observe patients and listen to their stories, both of dreams and of memories, to work out what was hidden in its depths.

However, Freud's structural model gave clues as to how the unconscious functioned, for here the id (source of the drives), guided by the pleasure principle, was considered to be unconscious, as was the superego (the introjections of parents' moral codes, societal norms, etc.). In fact, a greater part of the ego was also considered to be unconscious. What Freud could not do in terms of a detailed explanation for the unconscious, he could do for the conscious ego, thus adding to an understanding of some unconscious mechanisms. Ego creativity is probably that with which most of us are best acquainted. Let us therefore take a closer look at Freud's theory of the ego and conscious thought (the foundation for conscious creativity) and later move on to compare this with neuropsychological models of conscious thought, cognitive models and Lacanian theory. These will all hinge on the role of the body, which is (as we shall see) central to the process of creativity involving the ego.

The Project: perception, language and memory

Freud had, early in his career, written *Project for a Scientific Psychology* (1896) (largely based on neurology), which was published posthumously but had a strong influence on his writings and was particularly obvious in *Beyond the Pleasure Principle* (1920), which – amongst other writings – came to influence Lacan. The *Project* describes

> The cause of one's sometimes recollecting and sometimes not, though starting from the same point, is that from the same starting-point a movement can be made in several directions... It tends to move to the more customary:... Hence the rapidity with which we recollect what we frequently think about.
>
> (Aristotle 2001 [350 BC]: p. 614)

Freud's theory of memory, perception and conscious thought, as well as supplying psychoanalysis with a memory-based model of the ego.

The ego, according to Freud, is made up of a large network of energised (or cathected) nerves. Memories are established when intense external or internal events raise the energy levels within neurones. Kolb and Wishaw (neuropsychologists) describe a memory model very similar to Freud's using the metaphor of water being poured down a sand dune, producing grooves – deep ones where the force of water is greater and finer ones where the force of water is less. When more water is poured over the same area it will travel down the same grooves. Over time grooves which are used often become deeper and deeper. According to Freud, these are part of the ego's memory network.

Donald Hebb claimed that cells which fire together wire together. Freud had made this the foundation of his ego network model and its capacity to expand more than half a century earlier. A large network had the added benefit of being able to dissipate the damaging effect of traumatic events. Pain was considered to leave 'deeper grooves' and more facilitations than most other forms of excitation, and could therefore easily become reactivated, causing the memory to repeat with annoying regularity (as, for instance, when mulling over the memory of a recent loss). Having a large network would allow the flow of neuronal energy to quickly disperse down the many grooves of memory facilitations, a bit like watching the force of water fan out and dissipate through the many networks of grooves on a sand dune, thus avoiding repetition. In Freudian terms, the ego 'sets up' associations so as to be able to 'bind' incoming excitation and weaken neuronal flow. This will, for instance, occur if we talk about our problems, thus associating the traumatic event to the memory traces of the surrounding environment, the individuals with whom we are talking, the weather, the time of day, etc. This is also how new information comes to be integrated with existing memory systems, associations being 'set up' when the new information is repeated and related to previously memorised information (if, for example, I am learning about the reign of Elizabeth I, it is likely that I will associate some of the new information to knowledge I have about Henry VIII or Mary I, and repeat it for good measure).

What then is consciousness in Freudian terms? To answer this question we must look at how perception, language and memory interact.

Consider a child looking at an apple. According to Freud, the first encounter with the 'thing' or object (i.e. our first perception of something) lays down the blueprint for all other encounters. New encounters will be added to the original memory. The child will learn what an apple looks like by walking around it or lifting it up to the light, tilting it at various angles. S/he will probably both taste and smell the fruit and form an opinion of the experience (good or bad). Each observation (coupled with the response: good/bad) will be integrated into the memory traces pertaining to the original blueprint, along with the word for the object (apple). The word is essential in so far that, without words, our conscious perception of the world will be similar to hallucination. Words allow us to understand the quality of our perceptions. Further, they prime the brain to search out shapes and forms which correspond to it, i.e. once the child knows what an apple looks like and has a word corresponding to it, s/he will easily notice when apples are present amongst other fruits in a fruit bowl. The child will then know to avoid apples if necessary (they may have caused an allergic reaction) or to eat them if s/he is hungry and has formed a favourable opinion of the fruit.

The process of registering all experiences in terms of physiological reactions (pleasurable or unpleasurable) is also described by the neuropsychologist Damasio, who claims that these memories (along with registered responses of good or bad) are related to cognitive maps of the body and correspond to a 'basic ego'. Freud also argues that the ego is at first a 'bodily' ego, maps of associative memory traces (neurones) emerging from pleasurable and unpleasurable experiences with the body, related to the various erogenous zones that become activated at different points in the child's development (oral, anal, phallic, genital). The oral zone is of most importance during the child's first few years of life. The network of the ego, then, will contain a map of physiological responses in relation to the body and, for example, apple-eating. These memories, claims Damasio, also have an important function in facilitating correct social responses. To illustrate this, Damasio discusses the famous case of Phinneas Gage.

In the mid-nineteenth century, Phinneas Gage, a foreman working on the American railways, sustained a terrible injury while inspecting an explosive device that hadn't detonated. His company was attempting to blast its way through a rocky region in Vermont. Phinneas' brain was pierced by a metal pole which shot through the back of his cheek bone, severed the orbital nerve and exited through the frontal lobe with such force that it cauterised the wound and landed several metres away from the blast. Phinneas retained consciousness and could tell the doctor who treated him exactly what had happened. In spite of inflammation and ulcers, Phinneas survived and emerged a changed man – not in so far that his IQ was damaged (according to research), but rather in terms of EQ (emotional intelligence). Where Phinneas had, prior to the incident, been a courteous and conscientious man, he now became obstinate, irritable and not particularly well behaved around ladies. He left the railway and tried out a variety of jobs, many of which allowed him to travel. He later settled with his sister in Chicago, where he spent a great deal of time in the seedier parts of town. He finally died ten years later, due to complications caused by his wound. Damasio (1994) compared the change of personality seen in Phinneas (acquaintances who knew him before the blast claimed that he simply wasn't Phinneas any more) with patients suffering from lesions in the frontal lobes caused by tumours. Their behavioural changes were roughly similar and none suffered a registered change to IQ. Damasio claims that the cause of the change is a severing of communication between the frontal lobes (in charge of planning and rational thinking) and the parts of the brain responsible for storage of unconscious memories, as discussed above. Like Freud, Damasio claims that man registers all experiences from early childhood in terms of good and bad (which enables us to stay away from bad objects and stick to the good ones). It isn't possible or efficient to maintain these experiences as conscious memories (there are too many). Instead, these memories act 'unconsciously' to enable us to make efficient choices in social life. Social life, argues Damasio, is very complicated. To allow for our social life to run smoothly, our unconscious sorts away the worst choices (there are many) and serves our conscious memory with a handful of the best choices, allowing us to make very quick decisions – something that is necessary in order for humans to function well in a group (few people have time to wait while others sit and ruminate or vacillate over decision making). Damage to the frontal lobe (as seen in the case of Phinneas and several other cases described by Damasio) result in patients making one disastrous social choice after the next (Damasio claims that there are often more bad choices to be made than good ones and therefore when individuals with frontal lobe lesions choose, it is likely that the choice will be bad, having no unconscious sorting system). The importance of having access to the store of unconscious memories described above also becomes evident in research carried out by Roger Sperry (1964) on several commissurotomy patients (so-called 'split-brain' patients because the connection between the two hemispheres, *corpus callosum*, has been surgically severed), the results of which eventually led to him receiving the Nobel prize.

Sperry showed pornographic pictures to split-brain patients, only allowing the right hemisphere to process the information. The left brain is the primary locus of language (written language), but in split-brain patients communication between left and right hemispheres has been severed (to a greater extent). These patients reacted with embarrassment (indicating that the information had been processed) but could not explain what they had seen or why they were embarrassed. It would seem that Sperry's patients did have access to the unconscious source of socially correct choices and therefore responded as would be expected by somebody suddenly shown pornographic material in a hospital setting.

Sperry's research with split-brain patients implies that language affects how the individual processes, interprets and consciously understands his/ her perception (as does Freudian research). Freud sometimes referred to words as 'word images' and at other times as 'word motor images' (accentuating the importance of symbols in one case and movement in the other). Initially, however, consciousness is based on sound and perception according to Freud. The relationship between sound and perception is first brought about through the cry or scream of the baby.

The scream is the child's first form of communication, and therefore the first step towards language. It is also an indication of the quality of perception (ibid.: p. 367). Is it good or is it bad?

> In the first place, there are objects – perceptions – that make one scream, because they arouse pain; and it turns out as an immensely important fact that this association of a sound (which arouses motor images of one's own as well) with a perceptual [image], which is composite apart from this, emphasizes that object as a hostile one and serves to direct attention to the perceptual [image]. When otherwise owing to pain one has received no good indication of the quality of the object, the information of one's own scream serves to characterise the object.
>
> (Freud 1895: p. 366)

The scream refers to 'the first class of conscious memories', which in turn is related to pain (ibid.: p. 366). According to Freud, there are perceptions with sympathetic value, such as other people's pain, that will cause the subject to react by regenerating his own displeasure in relation to memories of pain. There are also perceptions that have an imitation value (ibid.: pp. 333–334). When a perception has an imitation value, it will cause the child to copy in his own mind the movements of the other human being by relating these to his own body (a process currently considered to be facilitated by mirror neurons). According to Freud, the basis for making a judgement about reality, which in turn results in an activity or a behaviour, involves 'the presence of bodily experiences, sensations and motor images of one's own' (ibid.: p. 333). Thus, the child will learn how to behave in relation to pain and pleasure by observing others and relating back to his own experiences. The child in the example above, who has never seen an apple, will, however, know how to respond to the fruit if it is bitter by wrinkling his/her nose or grimacing, as s/he has seen others do the same. In fact, the child can probably guess just by watching somebody else bite into the fruit whether it is bitter and if s/he will like it.

The mirror phase: through the looking glass of desire

Lacan's theory of the ego and conscious thought differs quite substantially from Freud's. The ego emerges during the mirror phase, according to Lacan. Lacan was inspired by Henri Wallon, a psychologist who was particularly interested in small children's relations to their mirror image, which he described as occurring from the age of 3–12 months. The rationale here is that recognition of a mirror image is indicative of self-awareness, just as in Gallup's tests, where chimps and other animals were placed in front of a mirror. A red spot had been placed on the animal's body, and the researchers observed if the animal understood that it was facing a reflection and whether or not it looked behind the mirror for another individual or responded with aggression. Lacan argued that man has not yet reached maturity when he meets his own image in the mirror. The image has what Lacan claims to be an 'orthopaedic' effect, supporting what is essentially an incoherent body. It is an imaginary sense of control (the ego belongs to the imaginary order, one of three orders in Lacanian theory). In this he was inspired by research within biology which focused on parenting. Many new-born animals are able to survive in nature without too much assistance from their parents, while new-born primates must cling to their parents for survival and sustenance, quite literally for months after birth. The image then promises a future of coherence and control; it is erotically attractive to the child.

... he had been taken, as a child, to see the mirror-room of the Panoptikon in Copenhagen, where you see yourself reflected, ... in a hundred glasses each of which distorts and perverts your face and figure in a different way – shortening, lengthening, broadening, compressing their shape, and still keeping some sort of likeness – and thought how much this was like real life. So your self, your personality and existence are reflected within the mind of each of the people whom you meet and live with. Even a flattering picture is a caricature and a lie.
(Blixen 2002 [1934]: p. 8)

The mirror image is the internal image the child has of himself, which he later projects on to the world, and in relation to which he understands his environment. Consciousness is discussed in relation to self-awareness in Lacanian theory. This is also located in the mirror stage and the emerging ego. Self-awareness is dependent on language, however. Here Lacan points to a specific event in the mirror phase (naming and the recognition of desire in 'other' children) as the moment when the child becomes self-aware:

> The subject originally locates and recognises desire through the inter-mediary not only of his own image, but of the body of his fellow being. It's exactly at that moment that the human being is conscious-ness, in the form of consciousness of self, distinguishes itself. It is in so far as he recognises his desire in the body of the other that the exchange takes place. It is in so far his desire has gone over to the other side that he assimilates himself to the body of the other and rec-ognises himself as body.
>
> (Lacan 1953–1954: p. 147)

Therefore, seeing another child (a younger sibling perhaps) suckling might cause the child to recognise his own desire in the other child's desire. Man is conscious of himself as body, then, because the other fel-low-being has made him so, according to the quote above. However, desire can only be recognised once it is mediated through language, according to Lacan.

This happens when the child encounters 'something' in the other that allows the subject to 'reproject' the ideal on to the other. In other words, when something in the other reminds the child of his ideal (based on the mirror image), desire becomes revived in the child, but now it is revived verbally (ibid.: p. 171). This is the moment when man becomes aware of his body and himself, which are essentially interlinked, according to Lacan. There is an 'I' and there is another: 'he has a body and I have a body'. This process eventually involves 'naming' as the child learns who the other is in relation to himself (ibid.: p. 155). Helen Keller became deaf and blind at the age of two and was taught sign language at the age of seven. In her book, *The World I Live In*, she claimed;

> When I learnt the meaning of I and me and found that I was some-thing I started to think. First then did I become conscious.
>
> (Keller 1909: p. 86)[1]

There would seem to be three different kinds of consciousness in Laca-nian theory: consciousness prior to the mirror stage; bodily self-awareness once the child has realised that the image in the mirror is its own; self-awareness (consciousness of one's own consciousness) once the child has recognised its desire in another child, coupled with naming. Is there any support for this 'series' of consciousnesses in neuropsychology and cogni-tive psychology?

A comparison between the neuropsychological and cognitive theories

Both neuropsychologists and cognitive scientists separate core consciousness or primary consciousness from reflective self-awareness (denoting the difference between being aware and being able to think about it). Core consciousness is something

> The permanent and abiding I (pure apperception) is the correlate of all our representations in so far as it is merely possible for one to become conscious of them, and all consciousness belongs to all-embracing pure apperception.
> (Kant 2000 [1781]: pp. 133–135)

we share with most animals, according to Damasio. It refers to the sense of being here and now. Consciousness (self-awareness in Lacanian terms) is dependent to a large extent on language, referring to the process of reflecting over one's thoughts and feelings. Gärdenfors also differentiates between primary consciousness (consciousness in Gärdensfors' terms) and secondary consciousness (self-awareness). When discussing secondary consciousness he presents Gallup's research and bodily self-awareness, but separates this from actual self-awareness, the latter being primarily human, dependent on autobiographic memory enriched by language. Gärdenfors argues that self-awareness is, at first, awareness of the other (as in Lacanian theory), which eventually becomes awareness of the self. Let us take a closer look at these theories.

Damasio and core consciousness

Consciousness according to Damasio (and other researchers in the field) is dependent on a network of nerves and small nuclei on the top of the brainstem at the base of the brain, which is often called RAS (reticular activation system) or simply RF (reticular formation). This network of nerves and nuclei get us up in the morning and helps us fall asleep at night. The nuclei in RF are, for instance, manipulated when people are put to sleep before an operation. The RF lies in conjunction with the area of the brain which receives information from the body, such as pleasurable or unpleasurable reactions to a variety of experiences, and regulates oxygen levels, blood flow and other important aspects of physical functioning. In this area a representative or map of the body will be stored (one of many in the brain), i.e. a rudimentary physiological self or ego.

However, the areas described above only allow for consciousness, not for the awareness of being conscious. The difference between these can be seen in people who have suffered brain damage. There are plenty of patients who are conscious, but they are not aware of being conscious and cannot respond or register anything going on in the outside world – a state many call vegetative (which is sometimes misconstrued as there are patients who don't seem to register information from the outside but are fully aware, as is the case in locked-in syndrome). Awareness of consciousness demands the involvement of two other areas of the brain. The thalamus is a relay area that registers stimuli coming from the outside world and sends the information to the cortex for analysis. It organises collective action in response to dangers and challenges, together with the amygdala and the limbic system in the middle brain. The other area of the brain necessary for awareness of consciousness is the Cingulate Cortex, which lies just above the limbic system. This area enables, for instance, attention and focus, but also organises motor sensory behaviour. Together, these two areas allow the brain to gauge the inner and outer world and create core consciousness. According to Damasio, we share core consciousness with most other animals.

Human consciousness, however, demands the involvement of language, working memory and autobiographic memory. Damasio claims that certain primates – and most probably some dogs – have autobiographic memories, but these are not as extensive and complex as those of a human being.

Gärdenfors and bodily self-awareness

Gärdenfors also differentiates between the experience of being here and now with that of being self-aware (Damasio's consciousness). Gärdenfors separates between sensations, perceptions and representations. Sensations rely on incoming stimuli; perception on processing stimuli; and representation on building incoming stimuli into internal representations of the external world. The latter can be used to create strategies for survival. Snakes, for instance, use their sensations during the hunt (sight for the kill and smell to find the dead prey). These sensations do not result in perception or inner representations, neither do the sensations cooperate, according to Gärdenfors. If, for instance, the snake cannot smell the newly killed prey, dinner is cancelled, even if the dead mouse is lying in front of the snake's eyes. A cat can hunt with the help of its representations. If its prey hides behind a rock, the cat knows (with the help of internal representations) that it is still there and so the cat can lie in wait for the mouse to break cover. It even has internal representations of how the prey behaves in different situations. Gärdenfors claims that this capacity to use inner representations is a characteristic of mammals and possibly even birds. Von Uxeküll claims that when prey runs to avoid a predator, it doesn't run from the stimuli of sound or sight, it runs from a mirror image of the predator which emerges in an internal mirror-world built on internal representations founded on perception.

> To the thinking soul images serve as if they were contents of perception (and when it asserts or denies them to be good or bad it avoids or pursues them). That is why the soul never thinks without an image.
>
> (Aristotle 2001 [350 BC]: p. 594)

Gärdenfors discusses bodily self-awareness in terms of Gallup's test. However, while chimps and orangutans have bodily self-awareness according to Gallup, they seem uninterested in how others perceive them, which is mainly a human preoccupation (hence a propensity for self-decoration that isn't visible in apes or primates). Consciousness of the body implies a capacity to focus on bodily experiences while being able to see yourself through the eyes of others, which, Gärdenfors argues, enables consciousness of consciousness (self-awareness). Citing Merleau-Ponty, he points out that the mirror image is important to self-awareness because it is through the mirror image that we understand how others see us. This argument is based on the importance of inner representations. Understanding the inner representation that others have of you enables you to see yourself from the outside. Further, Gärdenfors argues that there is nothing in research which implies that awareness of the workings of the 'inner' self develops earlier than the awareness of the workings of the other's inner selves – understanding what goes on in other people's minds probably develops before we understand what goes on in our own. The I (ego), then, is dependent on the other, argues Gärdenfors.

Gärdenfors argues that episodic memory, which enables autobiographic memory (a characteristic of the ego), is primarily human, as is the capacity to create narratives concerning internal events. While some chimps have language (taught in a laboratory setting), they do not, for instance, produce autobiographic accounts, so it is difficult to prove that they have a developed sense of an autobiographic self (their communication tends to centre around needs and external events rather than internal events).

Self-awareness, then, is dependent both on the ego (autobiographical self), the other and language. What consequences does this model have for the understanding of Lacan's views on knowledge (conscious knowledge)?

Connaissance: conscious imaginary knowledge

According to Lacan, man's experience of the surrounding world is constructed, in so far as his relationship to a 'knowledge' of the world is imaginary and dependent on the ego: 'Human knowledge and by the same token the sphere of relations of consciousness, consists in a certain relation to this structure that we call the ego around which the imaginary relation is centred' (Lacan 1954–1955: p. 177).

O Voltaire! O humaneness! O nonsense! There is something about 'truth', about the search for truth; and when a human being is too human about it – 'il ne cherche le vrai que pour faire le bien – I bet he finds nothing'.

(Nietzche 2000 [1886]: p. 237)

Damasio discusses the relationship between the neural patterns that arise in the brain as a response to perceptual processing in *The Feeling of What Happens*. He claims:

Thus the images you and I see in our minds are not facsimiles of the particular object, but rather images of the interactions between each of us and an object which engaged our organisms, constructed in neural pattern form according to the organisms design.

(Damasio 1999: p. 321)

Our images of the world, then, are constructed and to a degree even imaginary, according to Damasio. It is difficult to know what is 'really out there'. Damasio claims: 'I do not have any idea about how faithful neural patterns and mental images are, relative to the objects to which they refer' (ibid.: p. 320).

Lacan has a similar approach, though he is somewhat more radical. The real, claims Lacan, is unknowable ('impossible' in *Seminar XI*). There are several reasons for why Lacan chose such a stance. Kuhn had published *The Structure of Scientific Revolutions* in 1962; the epistemological debate was sharpening as to the status of scientific experiments in relation to producing a piece of truth about the world at the time. It was a debate which gained a great deal of attention and coverage (in books and articles) from the academic community and came to a head in 1965 when Popper and Kuhn met face-to-face at Bedford College, University of London. While Popper believed it was possible to formulate falsifiable hypotheses in relation to a specific scientific problem which would lead to a production of scientific knowledge, Kuhn claimed that all language is cultural, whereby every verbally produced hypothesis would ultimately yield culturally specific knowledge. Both, however, were in agreement on one point, we cannot reach truth with 100 per cent certainty, but we can do a great deal to get closer to it. Lacan, like Popper, gave natural sciences an elevated status in comparison to other sciences:

The world is segmented to the subject – the world of what I last time called thought is the equivalent, the 'mirror image' of thought. That is why there was nothing but fantasy regarding knowledge until the advent of most modern science.

(Lacan 1972–1973: p. 115)

Further, Lacan seemingly wanted to question all the self-serving beliefs that we hold in relation to our knowledge of the world and our tendency to believe that this knowledge is correct. He wanted to create a careful approach to knowledge, paving the way for the possibility to deconstruct and question knowledge as a natural part of creating knowledge. This sceptical approach to knowledge has a long history in the philosophy of science. Descartes was probably one of its most famous proponents, claiming the only thing he could really be sure of was that he existed. The British Empirical school, who's founder is often considered to be Bacon (the man who claimed that knowledge is power), and which also included Hobbes, Hume, Berkeley and Locke, is also famous for its radical scepticism. These philosophers discussed the problem of language in relation to knowledge, some claiming that language traps man in false pictures of the world (Bacon), and others claiming that we see the world as we do because of the words we use. Hume was probably the most radical of all, claiming that virtually nothing could be said with certainty about the outside world.

Summary

There are several important consequences of the Freudian theory described above. Before language, children develop cognitive maps in relation to external stimuli such as pain. These are motor-sensory, i.e. based on motor behaviours that the child can visualise internally. The internal manipulation of these maps provides the child with a variety of behavioural repertoires which can be used in relation to external stimuli and are directly related to the child's own body (as for instance with the child who has learnt how to express the sensation of 'bitter'). Once the child starts to connect sounds and words to memories, these (in combination with existing cognitive maps) will enable focal consciousness, i.e. consciousness geared towards understanding their external and internal environment, gauging them for objects which are pleasurable or noxious (e.g. good apple, bad apple). What we see and how we perceive our reality is based on what we already know and what we expect to see, which in turn is decided, amongst other things, by the individual's archive of words or signifiers. Memories are stored in a large network of nerves (as a potential for interaction between energised neurones), and these correspond largely to the conscious part of the ego. For memories to remain active in consciousness and easily accessible they must be used (e.g. eating apples or actively avoiding apples). The ego is originally a 'bodily' or corporeal ego, which eventually becomes a body of language. Consciousness, then, and retrievable knowledge of the world is dependent on the bodily self, memory and language.

The Lacanian ego is an imaginary construct based on the gestalt in the mirror that offers the child a sense of wholeness and control before it has actually reached this stage of coherency in its development. Language is necessary for conscious self-awareness to emerge, and it does so when the child recognises its own desire in another child's desire, its own desire for the breast in another child's desire for the breast. This (desire in the desire of the other), in combination with naming, allows the child to become conscious and self-aware.

Chapter 2

The symbolic order and the unconscious

Introduction

Freud claimed that very little could be said of the unconscious other than that it was the source of the drives and it contained a whole moral codex of society. However, the theory discussed in Chapter 1 allows us to say a few things of the unconscious. We know that it contains memories of perceptions connected to language and to a response (good/bad). Further, we know it contains maps of the body which are founded during childhood in response to the many experiences the child will have in the internal and external world. We know there are a mass of words in the unconscious and that the processes of condensation and displacement apparent in the dream content also exist within the unconscious. The unconscious is capable of closing off the functioning of limbs, and of plaguing us with unpleasant symptoms and underlying anxiety. Drives, instincts and the superego belong to the unconscious. But we also know the unconscious is capable of a great deal of creativity – creativity apparent in dreams.

> The inner world is so far for consciousness a bare and simple beyond, ... because in the void there is nothing known, or putting it from the point of view of the other side, because its very characteristic lies in being beyond consciousness.
>
> (Hegel 2003 [1807]: pp. 82–83)

In this chapter the symbolic order will be discussed, along with the subject of the unconscious. To do so I will present central concepts such as the law, desire, object *a* and *jouissance*. *Savoir* – knowledge belonging to the symbolic – will also be discussed and compared to *connaissance* – imaginary knowledge.

Language and the unconscious

Lacan claimed the unconscious is structured like a language. Lacan's interest in language and structure was influenced by the linguist Saussure and the social anthropologist Lévi-Strauss, who was a personal acquaintance. In the late nineteenth century Darwin was a strong influence on most sciences. Even within linguistics, researchers were busily charting family characteristics between languages in much the same way as biologists studied different species of animals and classified them according to similar characteristics. Saussure broke the trend. He claimed that language was built up by the *differences* between signifiers and sentences, not their similarities. It is, for instance, difficult to understand the concept of 'yellow' by placing a yellow object next to other yellow objects. Yellow is yellow because it isn't green or blue. It is in contrasting the yellow object with objects of other colours that we can arrive at an understanding of what yellow is. According to Saussure, the whole linguistic system is built on these contrasts. Further, the system corresponds to a linguistic structure involving different levels, governed by rules of grammar (laws) where signifiers (elements of language) within the system are defined by their relations to one another. Lévi-Strauss applied this idea to his research in social anthropology and found the kinship between people in the groups he studied could be understood in the same way.

But how does Lacan's subject come into the symbolic world?

Lacan, language and the body: birth, the first entry into the symbolic

Language affects the child before it is born in so far that the parents discuss what the child will be called, how parenting should proceed, where the child will sleep, etc. The parents bring their hopes and dreams to the birth of a baby and these act as a bedrock for

The essence of nature is now to be expressed symbolically; we need a new world of symbols; and the entire symbolism of the body is called into play, not the mere symbolism of the lips, face and speech.

(Nietzsche 2000 [1886]: p. 40)

the child's development. The child, then, is immersed in language at birth. Receiving its words from the Other, the child will learn to signify certain parts of the body when trying to explain pain and pleasure with signifiers obtained from the Other. In doing so, s/he must choose certain signifiers, which will belong to his/her semantic evolution. In this process the child will map and chart his/her own experiences of the body. S/he will experience this as a conscious process in so far that s/he is aware of his/her choice of signifiers during signification. The process belongs to the imaginary, but the elements s/he uses – the signifiers – will belong to the network of signifiers in the symbolic and will remain when memories of the process of charting are no longer available. Lacan claims, when discussing the unconscious in *Ecrits*, that the 'truth can be rediscovered' inter alia:

- in archival documents: these are my childhood memories, just as impenetrable as are such documents when I do not know their provenance;

- in semantic evolution: this corresponds to the stock of words and acceptations of my own particular vocabulary, as it does to my style of life and my character....

(Lacan 1966: p. 50)

Thus the symbolic body is related to the imaginary and dependent on it in so far as the child chooses to signify his/her experiences in a certain way. His/her 'style' will affect his/her semantic evolution, and the signifiers s/he chooses during signification will in turn be a part of his/her childhood experiences and memories. The body, then, is first and foremost a body of language: signifiers pertaining to the body hold certain positions in a linguistic structure that enable them to have meaning in relation to other signifiers. The imaginary body and the real body are only two aspects of the bodily ego (although the real body cannot be completely known). The symbolic body is the third.

We have seen already that the child's encounter with the mirror image positions the child's ego firmly in its imaginary world. Is there a similar moment when the child's symbolic world is set in place? To answer this question we will have to look at Lacan's theory of the Oedipus Complex. To do so I will briefly go through the Freudian theory, which will enable us to understand how Lacan developed his own perspective on the subject.

Freud, libido and the body: Oedipus, setting the symbolic firmly in place

Freud's developmental theory includes the oral, anal and phallic phases. During these, libido is directed towards a variety of erotogenic zones, the first being the mouth, the second the anus and the third the phallus, or genitals. The erotogenic zones give the child pleasure, according to Freud, and are therefore important throughout the child's development. Very small children tend to put things (most things they can get hold of) in their mouths; during the second year the child discovers the pleasure and attention involved in potty training. Repeated soiling can lead to many pleasant moments with the parent who changes and cleans the child. This, in turn, can be a welcome relief from boredom and loneliness, especially during sleepless nights. Successful potty behaviour can lead to accolades and appreciation. During the phallic phase children are excessively interested in genital differences between men and women, boys and girls. Children may also masturbate during this period. It is not unusual to see overtly sexual behaviour in Kindergarten, which can become quite disconcerting to staff who are relatively new to working with young children. Most of the time, however, the phallic phase is characterised by claims such as 'mine is bigger than yours', applied to a whole variety of settings.

The Oedipus Complex ends the phallic phase, which is somewhere around the child's fifth year, and refers to a period in development when a child desires one parent and tries to out-manoeuvre the other, according to Freud. Children can become excessively clingy in relation to one or the other parent, or even overly protective or assertive. It is not unusual to hear children claim that they intend to marry one or the other parent. However, the child eventually gives up his/her desire for fear of punishment.

According to Freud, fear of retribution causes castration anxiety. This is a reaction to the knowledge in boys that there are people who do not have penises, such as mothers and sisters. This leads to the realisation that a penis can be lost. The boy starts to fear retribution from his father due to his own sexual activities and his wish to 'own' his mother. The little girl's progress through the Oedipus Complex is not as clear cut, but in general little girls settle for the dream of having their own baby one day, according to Freud, giving up the desire for their fathers in the present in return for a baby in the future. Not all children desire the parent of the opposite sex or identify with parents of the same sex.

In Lacanian theory it is the mother's unmediated presence that causes the child anxiety (Lacan 1956–1957: p. 319). The mother's desire causes anxiety as the child asks itself what kind of object he is in her desire (Lacan reached this conclusion after working with psychotic patients). The child wonders whether or not he is disposable. In other words, would he be missed if he was suddenly lost (Lacan 1964: p. 214)? This is, for instance, evident when children try to visualise how their parents might react if they disappeared or ran away. The father intervenes during the Oedipal phase with the threat of castration, which may result in the child accepting the law against incest. Castration, then, is a protection against anxiety and not a cause, according to Lacan. The child is thereby separated from the mother and thus saved from anxiety.

The law, desire and *jouissance*

The law is a part of social exchange and necessary for social co-existence. However, the child has to sacrifice something when accepting the law.

> ... every impulse, and desire, and the rule over the whole animal is the domain of the soul.
>
> (Plato 1997 [360 BC]: p. 424)

The law demands that the child enjoys less. The child can, for instance, no longer enjoy his/her father or mother as s/he might wish – or anybody else for that matter (not until mutual consent is achieved in an adult relationship). A damper is put on pleasure, then, making childhood the lost paradise of long warm summers, endless days at the beach and sparkling white Christmases. It is this paradise or this capacity for enjoyment that man will attempt to re-experience through the various projects of his/her life. Some even go so far as to use chemical supplements to achieve and extend the same sense of pleasure.

Jouissance *and object a: desiring what others desire!*

The pleasure relinquished during the Oedipus Complex is called *jouissance*, and the lack which takes its place is represented by 'object *a*' in Lacanian theory. Object *a* is the object of desire. Hegel claimed that man desires what others desire (e.g. if my neighbour has a Mercedes, I want one). Lacan simply added that the subject desires what the Other desires (the unconscious dimension of the other), thus relocating the whole process of desire to the unconscious.

> The object of desire ... is the universal, ineradicable substance, the fluent self-identical essential reality.
>
> (Hegel 2003 [1807]: p. 104)

Consciously man believes that he 'knows' what he desires and strives to acquire these objects of desire. However, when his/her aim is achieved, the significance of the object (previously longed for) pales and eventually is replaced with new objects of desire. If I, for instance, dream of buying a new sofa and plan where I want it to be placed, buying it will probably make me happy for a while, but eventually it will simply 'become a part of the furniture' and I will probably start to plan for a new armchair, television or something else that I believe I am lacking. There will always be something I don't have and that I eventually will believe is absolutely necessary for my well-being. As I am driven by an unconscious desire and don't actually know what my object is (object *a*), I will, over time, try to fill my need (cover my lack) with a variety of objects, none of which will suffice.

The law then causes the subject (a desiring, lacking subject) to come into the realm of the symbolic, which represents the linguistic dimension, the structural laws of language. The law is represented by the fundamental signifier called the 'Name-of-the-Father' in Lacanian theory. The Name-of-the-Father acts as a master signifier (a kind of key word (S1) like the word 'God' in religious discourse), locking the relationship between signifier and signified into place. It comes to supply the quilting points for discourse (Lacan 1955–1956: p. 268). This moment (when the child accepts the law) is an equivalent to the moment of self-awareness of the mirror phase, when the child receives its orthopaedic image, promising control and mastery of itself in the world. Before the law is set in place, signifiers can slip and slide.

People with psychotic structures, for instance, can foreclose the law (according to Lacan), and when this happens their signifiers can start to slide in relation to the signified, taking on meanings of their own, creating new worlds of signification. Imagine excluding the word 'God' from the discourse of a deeply religious person! It would be extremely difficult to maintain a cohesive discourse. Schreber (a case study of psychosis described by Freud in 1911) foreclosed the law, according to Lacan, and developed a world peopled by birds, spirits, the rays of God, etc. after the onset of his second period of psychosis. Freud found that this world had a set of meanings all of its own (Freud 1911). When considering his psychosis, there would seem to be a proliferation of new metaphors. It would seem then that even in psychosis man does find a way of entering the symbolic – however, the relationship between signified and signifier slides. Words no longer mean what they once meant.

Accepting the law of the father doesn't only affect the symbolic body of words. It also has a very direct effect on the imaginary construct of the body. A severe consequence of foreclosing the law, for instance, can be seen when considering Schreber's relationship with his body. Freud claimed: 'He believed that he was dead and decomposing' (ibid.: p. 13). Schreber felt his body fragmenting during his delusions:

> During the first years of his illness certain of his bodily organs suffered such destructive injuries as would inevitably have led to the death of any other man: he lived for a long time without a stomach, without intestines, almost without lungs, with a torn oesophagus, without a bladder, and with shattered ribs, he used sometimes to swallow part of his own larynx with his food etc.
>
> (ibid.: p. 17)

The early phase of the mirror stage is caused by man's feelings of incoherence and fragmentation in relation to the 'whole' coherent ideal. However, the theory implies that the images of the fragmented body recede into the recesses of memory, into the archives of the symbolic (ibid.: p. 158), and are essentially *unconscious* once the child has passed through the Oedipus Complex. At this point the partial drives (which belong to the symbolic order in Lacanian theory) are gathered together into a 'shaky unity' with the internalisation of the Name-of-the-Father. After the Oedipus Complex, the body of the drives – the body which originally caused the subject to feel fragmented – should be acting in unity.

The ego-ideal, the Subject and the Other

When discussing the law during the early 1950s, Lacan was influenced by Claude Lévi-Strauss (Miller 1996). In this structuralist framework, language was very much understood as being bound up with a system of social exchange. The law is inherent to this system of exchange and refers

> Knudsen ... never in his narrations mentioned the name of a woman.... All the same when I was talking with him I felt in his life the constant presence of an unknown woman.... She was law and order embodied. In her claim of absolute power she had some likeness to the female deity of the Somali women.
>
> (Blixen 1989 [1937]: p. 149)

to fundamental principles underlying all social relations, making social coexistence possible. Hence, for instance, the location of the ego-ideal as belonging to the symbolic order (Lacan 1953–1954: p. 141). The ego-ideal, which in Freudian theory is the internalisation of significant 'others' in the child's environment, such his father and mother (i.e. people the child looks up to and wishes to be like), embodies the signifiers representing the law in Lacanian theory. The law sets limits on the subject and directs the subject to 'enjoy' as little as possible in Lacanian theory. The father is the law 'personified', also represented by the paternal metaphor (another of Lacan's linguistically oriented concepts), which describes the metaphoric character of the Oedipus Complex, where the Name-of-the-Father becomes a substitute for 'the desire of the mother' (the child desires the mother before the Oedipus Complex).

A young man came to Lacan because he could no longer use his hand. Lacan discovered that this young man had taken on the sin of his father (debts were inherited in the culture from which this young man came). He had heard his father, a civil servant who had lost his job, being accused of theft. The punishment for theft according to the legal system (an interpretation of Koranic law) in the young man's country of origin was to cut off the offending hand. The young man's inability to use his hand turned out to be caused by an internalisation of this law (represented by the signifiers 'off with his hand'). He had taken on his father's punishment (Lacan 1953–1954: pp. 196–198).

This brings us to the Other. The child receives its signifiers from the Other (in the case above, the father). When Lacan discusses the ego's relationship to other people he uses lower case letters to indicate that it is an imaginary relationship and is mainly achieved through projection (and see-sawing, as I will describe in Chapter 8). That is, the child sees himself in the other. When referring to the unconscious aspects of other people, Lacan uses upper case letters, i.e. the Other. The Other is both another human being and a place (the unconscious), an Other whom the child cannot fathom or understand, according to Lacan, in the Other's radical alterity. Here we sense the influence of Levinas' definition of the Other. The Other is non-assimilable, and any attempts at assimilation result in metaphysical violence. The Other is unconscious and symbolic. The first Other for both genders is the mOther. The mOther creates meaning from the child's attempts at early communication through punctuation, e.g. following up on the child's cries with an activity such as breast feeding, thereby assigning the child's cry with meaning. She is both the source of the signifier and the creator of meaning of the child's attempts at signification.

The unconscious symbolic dimension within each individual is called the 'Subject' (Lacan often uses the term interchangeably for the individual and for the unconscious symbolic dimension of the psyche). The term 'Subject' implies an active agent as opposed to a passive depository of repressed memories (and the Lacanian subject is indeed active). Therapy is directed towards the subject, whose 'speech' has 'profound' effects on the ego, according to Lacan. The 'subject' in philosophical discourse implies self-consciousness, and in legal discourse an entity answerable to the law and accountable for its actions. It is both in Lacanian theory (Evans 1996: p. 195). 'I think where I am not, therefore I am where I do not think' (Lacan 1966), Lacan writes in response to Descartes' 'Cogito Ergo Sum' – a quote that implies that the subject is a subject of thought! Thus 'I [the subject] thinks where I [the ego] is not' indicates that the ego's thinking is not stringent enough, as opposed to the subject's. But what is subjective thought? Can it be studied? I shall attempt to address these questions in the next chapter.

Knowledge and the symbolic order: *savoir*

Memory is related to the signifying chains of the symbolic order. Conscious memory is termed 'reminiscence' in Lacanian theory and is considered to be imaginary (Lacan 1953–1954: p. 59). Meaning, according to Lacan, is created along the chains of signifiers. Associative connections between signifiers and chains of signifiers enable the creation of new meaning (other than those represented in the signifier chains originally). There is a flexibility, then, which enables the development of 'new' meanings. The integration with other 'units of meaning' or other signifier chains enables new creative solutions to whatever problems the 'old' signifier chains might hold. Metaphor is central to this process. The signifier chains repeat, which becomes particularly obvious when the flexibility described above is lacking (due to a lack of metaphoric mediation), as can be seen in the traumatic dreams of PTSD, where the victim of trauma repeats the same scenario in nightmares night after night.

> Those thinkers in whom all stars move in cyclic orbits are not the most profound: whoever looks into himself as into vast space and carries galaxies in himself also knows how irregular all galaxies are; they lead into the chaos and labyrinth of existence.
>
> (Nietzsche 2000 [1882]: p. 175)

Metaphor lies at the heart of Lacanian theory. Lacan originally claimed that condensation refers to metaphor (Lacan 1966: p. 166) and displacement to metonymy (ibid.: p. 229). Metaphor enables man to 'store' more information than would otherwise be possible, but it also enables memory distortion and 'forgetting'. The presence of metaphor (many metaphors) in a discourse is normally an indication that discourse is flexible, which in turn results in the slow change of narratives over time (this is a central function of the symbolic and forgetting).

Lacan describes three different orders of knowledge; *connaissance*, *savoir-faire* and *savoir*. *Connaissance* refers to conscious knowledge and is dependent on the ego. While signifiers used by the ego belong to the symbolic, signification is imaginary and thus *connaissance* is dependent both on the symbolic and the imaginary, although it is primarily associated with the latter. *Savoir* belongs to the symbolic and is mainly unconscious. However, as we have seen, *savoir* can emerge in the classroom (e.g. in Parveen's lesson) or during therapy, after which it is integrated by the ego and becomes a part of *connaissance* – just as the signifiers cloaking *connaissance* can disappear into the archives of the unconscious and become subject to *savoir*. *Savoir-faire* is different to both orders and refers to know-how or physical knowledge which is not verbalised (in so far as it is related to the internalised schemata and representations of the body described in the previous chapter by Damasio and Gärdenfors, *savoir-faire* is both real and imaginary, though primarily associated with the real). It would, for instance, be very difficult to explain to somebody how to ride a bike, or perhaps how to successfully hit a hole-in-one without having any previous experience of golf. But before moving on to the next section I would like to add that it will become clear as this work progresses that *connaissance*, *savoir-faire* and *savoir* are all necessary for creative endeavour. *Savoir* often provides material for the creative endeavour, *savoir-faire* can provide the means for expressing the material, and *connaissance* allows for the material to be set into a context in which it can be experienced, understood and appreciated by others. All three orders of knowledge are necessary. I will, however, be focusing on *savoir* as it is a less well-known source of creativity and knowledge in the classroom. I believe that an in-depth understanding of this order of knowledge can bring positive changes to the classroom for both teachers and students, even if the path to this understanding can be long, winding and, in parts, rather steep.

Summary

The symbolic body comes into being through signification. With the help of signifiers the child eventually charts his/her body. How this is achieved depends on our primary caretakers and other significant adults in our environment who help us to name and describe various aspects of our own physical functioning. A small child can, for instance, seldom explain exactly where in the body s/he is experiencing pain. However, with time and assistance the child will be able to express the problem to the satisfaction of doctors and other adults.

The child comes into the symbolic dimension through the Oedipus Complex once the law of the father has been accepted. This law has very real consequences for the child. A child with a psychotic structure (who has never fully accepted the law) can, for instance, foreclose the paternal metaphor (the master signifier which locks discourse into place). Foreclosure may result in the experience of fragmentation (felt both as real and imaginary), as in the case of Schreber, described previously.

The symbolic, imaginary and real, then, are interlinked and in constant interaction. Therefore it would be true to say that the imaginary ego is shot through by the real and the symbolic, as we have seen with the imaginary body. Lacan calls the symbolic, the imaginary and the real 'orders' and depicts them as three interlinked hoops. The subject thinks when the ego is in doubt, Lacan claims. This implies that the subject comes into play in times of confusion, when the ego is faced with a problem it does not understand. Most of the time, however, the subject's thought only becomes accessible through therapy, dreams, slips of the tongue, jokes and repetition. I am going to investigate the hypothesis that creativity, especially of the kind described at the outset of this chapter, can be primarily symbolic and constituted by the subject. In order to do so, will discuss dreams in the next chapter.

Chapter 3

Dreaming and the subject of creativity

Introduction

Dreams are involuntarily creative, they can contain fragments and sometimes whole
sequences of memories which
are a repetition of the previous

Sleep that knits up the ravell'd sleave of care,
The death of each day's life, sore labour's bath,
Balm of hurt minds, great Nature's second course,
Chief nourisher in Life's feast.
(Shakespeare 1994a [1608]: p. 47)

day's activities interwoven with other material. They can be travelling
dreams, adventure dreams, nightmares or anxiety dreams. Some dreams
are repetitive, others thematic (the same theme reappearing in different
dreams over time). At times dreams are chaotic and at other times almost
prophetic. We may wake up feeling rejuvenated or utterly exhausted, but
one thing we can be sure of – as long as we live, a considerable percentage
of our lives will be spent dreaming.

Taking Freud's dream interpretation theory as a starting point, this
chapter presents current dream research and argues that creativity seen in
dreams is best understood in relation to the narrative of dreams (or the
'story teller'). Investigating the nature and origins of the 'story teller' so as
to better understand how this source of creativity might be used in the
classroom, the Descartian subject will be discussed in relation to the Lacanian subject, along with Plato's writings concerning creative thought in
Apology 22. Further, Schiller's thoughts concerning creativity are compared to Freud's (set out in the interpretation of dreams), and creativity
seen in visual arts and literature is discussed. Lacanian theory implies that
creative narrative is driven by the desire of the subject. This, in turn,
enables a discussion concerning the relationship between creativity, *jouissance* and pleasure seen in the classroom. Some of Lacan's pedagogic methodologies are presented along with what these might bring to the
understanding of creative reading as described by Bergstedt (1998). The
relationship between fantasy, desire and creativity, and methodologies for
working with creativity in the classroom are presented briefly at the end of
the chapter.

The subject of dreams

Freud discussed dreams in many of his case studies. However, his first 'best seller' was *The Interpretation of Dreams*, which was originally published in 1899 (though the date on the title page was 1900). For Freud, dreams were the royal road to the unconscious. They expressed

... the dream experience has been embodied by the Greeks in their Apollo ... the sooth-saying god.... The higher truth, the perfection of these states in contrast to the incompletely intelligible every day world, this deep consciousness of nature, healing and helping in sleep and dreams ... which makes life possible and worth living.
(Nietzsche 2000 [1886]: p. 35)

wish fulfilment. The dream content was a cloaked and disguised version of repressed wishes expressed unconsciously during 'day dreaming' mixed with residual memories (mainly from the previous day). The disguise of repressed wishes was made possible by the process of displacement and condensation according to Freud, which I will now go on to discuss.

Freudian dream theory: piecing together the script

Freud described the case of the Wolfman in 1918, and in this description included a segment of a dream which involved the Wolfman looking out of his window and seeing wolves sitting in a tree. In discussing the dream, Freud discovered that the Wolfman's grandfather had told him a story about a fox that had lost its tail to the hunter's knife. The Wolfman suffered from castration anxiety, according to Freud, and the story had come to represent castration for the child.

The fox of the story is replaced by several wolves in the dream. Because of the many associations between words and sentences, meaning can shift and slide along an associative signifier chain: e.g. fox, wolf, dingo, wild dog, hyena, tiger, lion. The original concept, 'fox', becomes *displaced* along the signifier chain. Freud uses the 'on', 'off' aspect of tails as an indication of castration anxiety, which is yet another example of displacement, but also of condensation (a symbol or a dream segment having many meanings). The wolves' tails represent phalluses, which have not been detached. The appearance of many wolves with firmly attached tails is an expression of wish fulfilment, i.e. the denial of the Oedipal threat (there are tails/phalluses which don't fall prey to the hunter's/father's knife and therefore I may go on desiring my mother or father or both).

In discussing dream content, Freud claimed:

> The dream is not comparable to the irregular sounds of a musical instrument, which instead of being played by the hand of a musician, is struck by some external force; the dream is not meaningless, not absurd, does not presuppose that one part of our store of ideas is dormant while another part begins to awake. It is a perfectly valid

psychic phenomenon, actually a wish-fulfilment; it may be enrolled in the continuity of the intelligible psychic activities of the waking state; it is built up by a highly complicated intellectual activity. But at the very moment when we are about to rejoice in this discovery a host of problems beset us. If the dream, as this theory defines it, represents a fulfilled wish, what is the cause of the striking and unfamiliar manner in which this fulfilment is expressed? What transformation has occurred in our dream thoughts before the manifest dream, as we remember it on waking, shapes itself out of them? How has this transformation taken place? Whence comes the material that is worked up into the dream?

(Freud 1900: p. 33)

Whence indeed! It cannot be the censor (which guards and protects preconsciousness and consciousness from unconscious desires and wishes), for when Freud discusses one of the poet Friedrich Schiller's letters (addressed to his friend Körner, who was having problems with his creativity), it is precisely the relaxation of the censor or the critical agent which makes creativity possible (Freud 1895: pp. 14–15). When discussing the role of the censor, Freud claims:

This function proceeds in a manner which the poet maliciously attributes to the philosopher: with its rags and tatters it stops up the breaches in the structure of the dream. The result of its efforts is that the dream loses the appearance of absurdity and incoherence, and approaches the pattern of an intelligible experience. But the effort is not always crowned with complete success. Thus, dreams occur which may, upon superficial examination, seem faultlessly logical and correct; they start from a possible situation, continue it by means of consistent changes, and bring it – although this is rare – to a not unnatural conclusion. These dreams have been subjected to the most searching elaboration by a psychic function similar to our waking thought; they seem to have a meaning, but this meaning is very far removed from the real meaning of the dream.

(ibid.: pp. 351–352)

It would seem from the quote above that dreams are made up of a variety of segments that have been 'disguised' before the censor forges them together into coherent dreams. The censor is also a part of consciousness that can comment critically on the dream while it is in progress, claiming: 'After all it is only a dream' (ibid.: p. 350). However, underlying the manifest dream content are cohesive segments of dream scenarios which, like the various acts of a theatre play, eventually become rewritten by a movie scriptwriter (through condensation and displacement) and are put together into a film (by the censor). Who or what, might we ask, writes the play (as opposed to the movie scriptwriter), casts the roles, arranges the props and theatre backdrops?

Let us take a look at current biological models of dreaming to see how these compare to the Freudian model above, and whether they might provide any answers as to how the dream is constructed.

Dream theory, biology and neuroscience: neurotransmitter theory, A–S theory and the cortical model

Dream research includes several models describing the biology of dream formation, such as the neurotransmitter model, electrophysiology model, activation–synthesis theory and cortical theory, which will be described here briefly as they have consequences for the understanding of Lacanian and Freudian dream theory.

We can best obtain a scientific view of the nature of the dream and the manner in which it originates by regarding it in the light of the circumstances attending sleep. The objects of sense-perception corresponding to each sensory organ produce sense-perception in us, and the affection due to their operation is present in the organs of sense not only when the perceptions are actualized, but even when they have departed.

(Aristotle 2001 [350 BC]: p. 620)

Hartman (1984) discusses a neurotransmitter model where the interrelation between a decrease in the release of serotonin and norepinephrine on the one hand, and an increase of dopamine and acetylcholine on the other, explains the initiation and the end of REM dreaming. This model, however, does not explain the presence of non-REM dreaming (nightmares seen in patients with PTSD occur during non-REM sleep according to Kramer (2007).

Winson (1990) presents a theoretical model based on electrophysiology (developed from animal research with subprimates). Dreaming, argues Winson, helps animals in the creation of behavioural strategies for survival, as well as to compare occurrences in the external world with these strategies, which in turn, argues Winson, might be used as a model for human dreaming. Winson claims that REM sleep has an evolutionary role and that this can be illustrated by the fact that anteaters (monotremes) do not dream, while after the split between monotremes on the one hand, and marsupials and placentals on the other (140 million years ago), dreaming became evident (Winson equates dreaming with REM sleep). Winson claims that theta waves and spatial memory are related and points to Foulkes' (1982) findings that children start to report dreams when their spatial skills appear. However, theta rhythms do not appear in the hippocampus of humans, and it is questionable if we can transfer the theory across species.

There are two major competing theories in neuroscience when considering the functional anatomy of dreams. One is put forward by Hobson *et al.* (2000), the so called A–S theory or activation–synthesis theory, and the other, cortical theory, is put forward by Solms (1997). According to the first theory, PGO (ponto-geniculate-occipital) waves are discharged at random from pons in the brain stem to the cortex. The cortex responds by trying to elaborate on these, albeit in a rather passive way. The model for dreams is delirium as seen in patients. The brain tries to make the best of incoming information and relies on affect accompanying the random discharge of PGO waves.

However, according to Kramer (2007), many dream researchers put forward evidence illustrating that dreams are more orderly and mundane than chaotic (for instance, Snyder (1970); Heynick (1993)). Snyder collected records of a large amount of dreams during laboratory research. Heynick studied speech in dream reports and found that in most cases the grammatical and syntactical structure was intact, as opposed to deconstructed and chaotic. Kramer discusses research which shows that certain types of dreams are reported amongst a variety of different populations, such as 'falling', 'being pursued' and 'object endangered', which indicates that dreams are not just random as the A–S theory implies. Gahagan (1936), for instance, handed out dream questionnaires to 559 students at a college and found that 87 per cent had experienced the falling dream, 64 per cent being pursued by a person, and 62 per cent being pursued by an animal. Griffith et al. (1958) handed out a questionnaire to 473 college students and 78.9 per cent reported they had experienced the falling dream and 83.5 per cent the attack/pursued dream. Kramer et al. handed out a questionnaire to a random sample of the population in the city of Cincinnati. Of these, 51.9 per cent reported dreams involving a 'person or thing under threat'. Further, Kramer has found that there are patterns of dream content which can be accounted for by differences in demography, gender, age and social status.

The cortical theory is based on the study of patients with localised brain lesions affecting their capacity to dream. Patients having experienced lesions affecting the centre source for seeking, wishing and desiring behaviour (an area involving fibres from the ventral tegmental area of Tsai, also connected to the limbic structures) report a loss of dreaming (or the experience of dreaming). This is also the case for patients who have lesions affecting areas of the brain involving spatial orientation and symbolic activity (inferior parietal area of either side of the brain). According to this theory, dreaming is not the equivalent of REM sleep. REM sleep is seen to initiate dreams, as is noise. Solms argues that dream imagery is constructed from memory and is not a simple reproduction. Hobson et al. have criticised Solms' theory, claiming that patients with lesions can recover their capacity to dream and therefore the results of dream research carried out with such patients must be questioned.

The cortical theory has, however, several interesting consequences when considering Freudian and Lacanian models. First, it places the initiation of dreams in areas which are in charge of seeking, wishing and desiring behaviour, which would imply that wish fulfilment is a motivating force in the dream process, as is claimed by Freud. The added findings from Kramer's own research, taken together with results presented by Gahagan and Griffith, support Freud's description of classical dreams such as 'falling', 'being pursued', 'object endangered' and dreams of embarrassment, such as being seen naked. Further, dreams are constructed actively (according to the cortical theory), involving both visual association areas as well spatial and symbolic activity, which leaves open the possibility of dream narrative (central to Lacanian theory) as a driving force of the dream. Kramer states that one of the problems of the A–S model is that the narrative structure of the dream is not addressed, and cites Foulkes' (1999) claim that the narrative is one of the dream's foundations.

The story teller

The importance of narrative and the claim that dreams are ordered as opposed to chaotic implies that there is a 'story teller' located somewhere in our psyche, and that this story teller is not open (most

> The beautiful illusion of the dream worlds, in the creation of which every man is truly an artist, is the prerequisite of all plastic art, and as we shall see, of an important part of poetry also.
>
> (Nietzsche 2000 [1886]: p. 34)

of the time) to intervention from our normal consciousness or ego. However, the story teller is aware of 'order', what makes a good story, what roles should be applied to the 'I' of the dream, etc. It is a lucid, intelligent and creative story teller that weaves narratives every night, for all of our lives! Sometimes, however, it runs out of themes and throws in a good car chase or a 'being pursued' section like so many authors of thrillers and detective novels. Alternatively, it might add a comedy act, with us turning up at work naked. Then, of course, there is sex and violence (which, according to Kramer (2007: p. 66), is mainly seen in male dreamers).

Let us turn to Lacanian theory, where the dream narrative is central to the dream, in an attempt to discover if it might enlighten us as to the unconscious mechanisms of the dream narrative.

Dreaming and desire: behind the mask of the dream

In Lacanian theory the dream is driven by desire – the subject's desire. This is interesting in so far as Lacanian theory would seem to imply that the dream narrative is permeated by pleasure. The claim is surprising, however, if we consider the common nightmare. There would seem to be very little pleasure derived from traumatic dreams.

When discussing the dream and desire, Lacan actually chose a nightmare caused by a current event. In *The Interpretation of Dreams* (1900),

Freud had described the dream of a man whose son had died from fever. The son revisits him in a dream with the reproach: 'Father, can't you see I am burning.' The man awakes to find that his son's body is indeed burning in the adjoining room because a candle has set the bed alight. The father has been traumatised by the death of his son. The chance encounter with the real is the smell of smoke coming from the adjoining room, which does not immediately wake him. He has not seen his son's body on fire, but the smell of smoke and the recent loss of his son to fever are integrated into an image of his son tugging at his arm, reproaching him (ibid.: p. 509).

This dream is significant because it enables Lacan to describe an immediate response by the psyche to a chance encounter with the real (the smell of smoke), integrating it into an ongoing dream so that the dreamer need not awake. The traumatic event is subject to *metaphoric mediation* in that the father dreams not of smoke, but of his own child reproaching him with the words: 'Father, can't you see I am burning.' Condensation, then, is the underlying mechanism of dream distortion and not the result (it would seem) of an attempt to disguise unacceptable wishes. Or is it? The dream enables Lacan to state that the dimension of desire is always present – even in traumatic dreams – as we shall see.

Discussing the trauma of the dream, Lacan puts the problem in a rather enigmatic way (which is typical of Lacanian pedagogy):

> Our experience then presents us with a problem, which derives from the fact that, at the very heart of the primary processes, we see preserved the insistence of the trauma in making us aware of its existence. The trauma reappears, in effect, frequently unveiled. How can the dream, the bearer of the subject's desire, produce that which makes the trauma emerge repeatedly – if not its very face, at least the screen that shows us that it is still there behind?
>
> (Lacan 1964: p. 55)

Here we have an example of one of Lacan's creative riddles. When I first read this, I set to work going through the whole of *Seminar XI* (several times). I was not disappointed. Lacan nearly always provides us with a solution to his riddles, which is why I am not prone to agreeing with Felman's claim that Lacan's texts are riddles unto himself (in Todd 1997). However, it demands a great deal of non-sequential jumps in the text and patience. Lacan states that the desire of this particular dream manifests itself 'by the loss expressed in an image' (Lacan 1964: p. 59), the image being his son. This loss would at first seem to be obvious. The dreamer has lost his son, who now revisits him in the dream. But Lacan suggests that the dream is *the screen for another reality*. There is something behind the screen, which he indicates by the statement that the dream is 'the bearer of the subject's desire'. When discussing the dream in an earlier chapter,

Lacan states that the child of the dream burns with the sins of the father (ibid.: p. 34). Following this argument, the child of the dream thus represents the dreamer himself – but then what is lost, if not the child? (Lacan claims that, as in any dream, the *ego* dissolves in the nightmare and the *subject* appears distributed amongst the various personae in the dream scenario (ibid.: p. 51).) Let us investigate Lacan's claim that the child of the dream (representing the father) is burning up with sin or with *jouissance* (pleasure in this instance), which is related to desire. To do so, we must first look at Lacan's concept of *jouissance*.

Jouissance *and dreams: on eating strawberries*

Jouissance in Lacanian theory is either pleasure or (when the subject has gone beyond the pleasure principle) a mixture of pleasure and pain. As in Freud's early writings, the pleasure principle is a homeostatic device that maintains a low level of tension in the psychic apparatus. It is an effect of the chains of signifiers and belongs to the realm of the symbolic (as discussed in Chapter 1).

> The function of the pleasure principle is, in effect, to lead the subject from signifier to signifier, by generating as many signifiers as are required to maintain at as low level as possible the tension that regulates the whole functioning of the psychic apparatus.
>
> (Lacan 1959–1960: p. 119)

For instance, when the young Anna Freud dreams of eating strawberries, which she had been denied, she was using the signifiers pertaining to 'strawberry eating' to conjure up the memory of the desired objects and thereby achieve a wish fulfilment, which in turn reduced tension (Freud 1900: p. 130). This theory also explains why talking about problems reduces tension. Talking is 'in effect, to lead the subject from signifier to signifier'!

Excess *jouissance* is 'given up' during the Oedipus Complex. The child might desire his mother or his father, but the law puts a limit on what and who may or may not be desired. Once the child has accepted the law against incest, there is also a limit put on enjoyment. The child cannot 'enjoy' others sexually or enjoy his own aggression (sometimes coupled with sadistic impulses) as the law limits his behaviour towards others. However, the *jouissance* or enjoyment lost does not disappear, according to Lacan, but is relegated to the real (Lacan 1964: p. 205) and is represented by object *a*, as it is lacking (Lacan 1962–1963: Chap 14, p. 10).

Jouissance lost to the real may, to a degree, be illustrated by the fantasy of other people in other places enjoying themselves more than we do (the idea that 'the grass is always greener'), or the belief that there is superabundant *jouissance* somewhere else in the world (Žižek 1998: p. 210). Object *a* is an effect of the internalisation of the law, when it divides the subject (\$) and causes it to desire because of the *jouissance* or enjoyment lost. It is possible, then, that the child of the dream represents not only a loss per se, but is burning up with lost *jouissance* – object *a*, the object of desire and anxiety – and therefore represents the dreamer and not the dead son. The dream, then, is only partially associated to the current event (the death of a child); it represents the memory of unacceptable desire! Dreaming, desire and pleasure are therefore interrelated whether the dream be a nightmare or not.

The dream discussed above is not particularly elaborate. The secondary revision described above has not caused the dream content to veer far off from the cause of the dream. In 'Father, can't you see I am burning', the dead son is exchanged for a living son, the smell of smoke is transformed into the word 'burning'. The dream masks the unacceptable wish expressed in the dream. Many dreams are a great deal more creative than the two dreams described above, and probably a great deal more indicative as to what secondary revision can achieve given a wealthy foundation of unconscious material. They can involve trips to foreign countries or adventure themes.

The subject, then, is an active agent, a *story teller*. It is aware of what makes a good story, what roles should be applied to the 'I' of the dream. It would seem to be a lucid, intelligent and creative story teller, which weaves narratives every night, forcing us to play leading roles – sometimes several – but with no greater cost to ourselves other than the pleasure or displeasure caused by the dream plot (unless we are beset with nightmares). The subject is obviously a potential source of creativity. However, it doesn't normally speak outside of therapy, according to Freud and Lacan, which presents us with a problem when considering the possibility of being able to access the subject's creativity during classroom activities.

Let us return briefly to the example of classroom creativity discussed at the outset of this book. Could the steady flow of creative answers during Parveen's lecture in anyway be related to the subject? If so, why did we experience our own answers as nonsensical while Parveen immediately recognised them as important contributions to future thesis chapters? (The story teller's activity is supposed to be lucid and intelligent according to the theory discussed above.) These are questions that need to be addressed before we move on to look at creative activities in the classroom, such as painting, writing and reading, along with creative exercises based on Lacanian theory. To do so I will discuss creative thought and the subject within the context of therapy. While the therapeutic setting is not directly translatable into a classroom setting, it may illuminate certain aspects of subjective speech that can be used by teachers and students.

Creative thought and the subject

Complex dreams demand complex thought (and not only creativity). In discussing Descartes' subject of certainty ('I think therefore I am'), Lacan claimed 'I think where I am not', and in considering Descartes'

... I is the condition of the predicate 'think'. It thinks; but that this 'it' is precisely the famous old 'ego' is, to put it mildly, only a supposition, an assertion, and assuredly not an 'immediate certainty'.

(Nietzsche 2000 [1886]: p. 214)

subject of doubt ('I doubt therefore I think'), Lacan claimed 'I think only when in doubt'. Lacan argues that it is Freud who introduces this dissymmetry with the Descartian subject, placing thought in the unconscious.

> In short, he is sure that this thought is there alone with all his I am, if I may put it like this, provided, and this is the leap, someone thinks in his place. It is here that the dissymmetry between Freud and Descartes is revealed. It is not in the initial method of certainty grounded on the subject. It stems from the fact that the subject is 'at home' in this field of the unconscious. It is because Freud declares the certainty of the unconscious that the progress by which he changed the world for us was made.
>
> (Lacan 1998 [1964]: p. 36)

Lacan thus considers the 'thinking subject' to be Freud's greatest achievement, de-seating the ego, as a primary locus of intervention and inquiry of psychology. It is precisely in the dream that we can observe the subject's thoughts usurping the place of 'I am'. 'I am' is determined by the subject who assigns the roles and creates the narratives. The subject thinks in the ego's place, or rather 'I think where I am not' as Lacan claims in *Ecrits*. This might seem to be a problem when considering classroom activities which rely on some kind of 'mastery' of thought. The Lacanian subject cannot be mastered. Further, it not only thinks, it speaks (mainly in therapy). An uncontrollable thinking subject might be thought of as a problem by some and an uncontrollable speaking subject as quite intolerable by others. But let us first consider what Lacan means by the thinking, talking subject within the context of therapy, where the subject's thoughts are expressed in the presence of an analyst.

Therapy was originally carried out with the help of free association in Freudian psychoanalysis. The flow of speech achieved during therapy is not merely creative, it is also meaningful and cohesive (as in the dream above); otherwise therapists would be dealing with something reminiscent of psychotic speech. In the *Interpretation of Dreams*, Freud discusses creativity and cites the abovementioned letter from Schiller to Körner. Freud later likens the process described by Schiller to free association as used in therapy.

The reason for your complaint lies, it seems to me, in the constraint which your intellect imposes upon your imagination. Here I will make an observation, and illustrate it by an allegory. Apparently it is not good – and indeed it hinders the creative work of the mind – if the intellect examines too closely the ideas already pouring in, as it were, at the gates. Regarded in isolation, an idea may be quite insignificant, and venturesome in the extreme, but it may acquire importance from an idea which follows it; perhaps in a certain collection with other ideas, which may seem equally absurd, it may be capable of furnishing a very serviceable link. The intellect cannot judge all these ideas unless it can retain them until it has considered them in connection with these other ideas. In the case of a creative mind, it seems to me, the intellect has withdrawn its watchers from the gates, and the ideas rush in pell-mell, and only then does it review and inspect the multitude. You worthy critics, or whatever you may call yourselves, are ashamed or afraid of the momentary and passing madness which is found in all real creators, the longer or shorter duration of which distinguishes the thinking artist from the dreamer. Hence your complaints of unfruitfulness, for you reject too soon and discriminate too severely.

(Schiller, letter 1 December 1788, in Freud 1895: pp. 14–15)

Freud goes on to claim:

And, yet such a withdrawal of the watchers from the gates of the intellect, as Schiller puts it, such a translation into the condition of uncritical self-observation, is by no means difficult. Most of my patients accomplish it after my first instructions. I myself can do so very completely, if I assist the process by writing down the ideas that flash through my mind. The first step in the application of this procedure teaches us that one cannot make the dream as a whole the object of one's attention, but only the individual components of its content.

(ibid.: p. 15)

Freud was of course referring to free association (a technique which is often used inadvertently by teachers as a part of competitions, charades and other similar exercises). In Lacanian therapy, a dialogue with the analysand is achieved by being 'dead enough', i.e. by avoiding the ego's (the analysand's) censorious response, which is often characterised by narcissism (feelings of love and hate projected on to the therapist). The analyst aims to speak directly to the subject by circumventing the ego (exercises which do not lead to competition between individuals in the classroom, for instance, might have a similar effect as will be discussed in Chapter 8). Therapy, however, is seldom a smooth ride. In fact, it is quite the opposite. The subject more often than not shows itself through gaps and disruptions (memory lapses, resistance, etc.) in the analysand's discourse. Smooth, long dialogues with the subject do exist, but they are a luxury appearing more and more often towards the end of therapy. How, then, does the analyst achieve knowledge in relation to the fragments of signifiers produced by the subject?

Savoir *and creativity in the classroom: I think where I am not*

When discussing the relationship between truth and knowledge of the unconscious, Lacan argues; 'How can we know without knowing? It's an enigma! ... which is a property of truth–truth can only ever be said by halves.' Lacan then goes on to liken truth to the

> ... the aesthetically sensitive man stands in the same relation to the reality of dreams as the philosopher does to the reality of existence: he is a close and willing observer, for these images afford him an interpretation of life, and by reflecting on these processes he trains himself for life.
>
> (Nietzsche 2000 [1886]: p. 34)

chimera's riddle given to Oedipus: 'I think you can see what the functions of the enigma means – it's a half said, just as the chimera appears as half-body.' Finally, Lacan puts the analyst into the picture: 'An enigma is most likely that, an utterance. I charge you with the task of making into a statement' (Lacan 1969–1970: p. 36). The analyst must then take all signifiers coming from the analysand and make sense of these to arrive at the truth. True speech is a creative process, as is interpretation.

The implications for the classroom are that a methodology eliciting subjective creative speech will, in turn, elicit creativity from the interpreter of this speech. Subjective speech may be seemingly lucid and meaningful, but it is often non-contextual, and at times even non-sequential, and doesn't necessarily make sense to the speaker even though it 'feels right'. The teacher's own creative capacity will be brought to bear on the students' creative speech when using poststructuralist methodologies. This might seem 'mysterious' or difficult to achieve. However, the same dimension of creativity can also be found in the interpretation of poems, according to Lacan.

Socrates discusses the work of poets in Plato's *Apology* 22, and claimed that when asked, they could not interpret their own poetry. Socrates then goes on to claim that the work of poets is similar to that of diviners. They speak but do not understand the meaning of their own divination. It is up to the reader to make sense of the poem. This may appear to be overly simplistic. Teachers are not therapists and students' creative speech is not to be understood or treated in the same way as an analysand's creative speech. In other words, we are not in the classroom to delve deeply in our students' psyches, and therefore the deep dimensions of the unconscious present in creative speech are neither of immediate interest or importance to the classroom. These dimensions affect the students' development subliminally, so to speak. However, the creative forms that subjective speech takes are important in so far that these can lead to the development of new thesis chapters, essays and other similar classroom activities.

As for subjective speech, Lacan claims paradoxically: 'What the subject fears most is to mislead us, to put us on the wrong track' (1981: p. 37). It is eager to speak, to find solutions. The half-truths or non-sequential, non-contextual jumps in speech, then, might not be too challenging or diffuse, and so perhaps the prospect of an uncontrollable speaking subject is not so intolerable or impossible after all.

There are situations which set the subject's creativity in motion, according to Lacan. For instance, when the subject is faced with the object of desire, or when the subject is faced by the Other's desire (the teacher can position him/herself as both, as will be discussed in Chapter 4). In therapy the analyst takes the position of object *a*, and so the subject's desire is set in motion (we desire what we lack), producing signifier after signifier (in much the same way Parveen positioned herself in the example discussed earlier). Taking the position of object *a* is often related to 'being the expert', or in Lacanian terms, the 'subject supposed to know'. Creativity elicited by the Other's desire refers to the unconscious dimensions of other individuals. If the Other's desire is interpreted in such a way that the student registers (unconsciously) that the teacher expects him/her to achieve, this will also set the subject's creativity in motion. Being caught in the Other's desire is related to the gaze, i.e. the experience of having been seen or of being seen.

When applying the theory discussed above to Parveen's lecture, it would indeed seem that the creativity elicited was that of the subject. Lacanian theory confused us. We were often confronted with what seemed to be riddles and half-truths. In asking us to discuss what we had read and what we had learnt during the lecture, Parveen was expecting us to achieve something which seemed almost impossible for many of us at the time. We didn't want to show our ignorance and believed we could have made sense of the reading and the lecture if only we had tried hard enough. When Parveen asked us to explain something our egos could not deal with, there was a bursting of our dams. Quite literally, our subjects took over, an experience very close to that of Schiller's description. Our answers and ideas really did rush through 'pell-mell'. It was followed by a feeling of exuberance, a rush which was quite dizzying when combined with the realisation that we were actually saying something important. My first thesis chapter was based on creative ideas that emerged during this experience.

There is a difference, then, between ego creativity – which is what we normally associate with creativity in the classroom – and the creativity of the subject. Both are important to the creative process in general. How might we as teachers approach creativity in the classroom, considering the theory discussed above?

Let us return to Schiller's letter so as to obtain some indication of what might be important when attempting to facilitate creativity of the subject in the classroom. When addressing Körner's concerns, Schiller states: 'The reason for your complaint lies, it seems to me, in the constraint which your intellect imposes upon your imagination' (Schiller, letter 1 December 1788, in Freud 1895: pp. 14–15). We are used to our intellectual work providing the main and most important source of creativity in the classroom. Intellectual work demands control, critical thinking, systematic thinking and the creation of meaning. All of these activities belong mainly in the domains of the ego and superego; both are detrimental to the creativity of the subject. It is most important, then, for any teacher attempting to work with the creativity of the subject to avoid the censorious response of the ego. There are exercises which specifically address the critical agent in teachers and students, toning down this tendency as an expressed part of the activity, such as Jack Norin's creativity exercises, which will be discussed in the chapter concerning methodology.

Schiller claims:

> In the case of a creative mind, it seems to me, the intellect has withdrawn its watchers from the gates, and the ideas rush in pell-mell, and only then does it review and inspect the multitude.... Hence your complaints of unfruitfulness, for you reject too soon and discriminate too severely.
>
> (ibid.)

The implication here is a 'giving up' of control, something many teachers feel uncomfortable with in the classroom. We are managers as well as teachers, and as such we have a responsibility for what happens in our classrooms. Relinquishing control in classrooms with younger students can be a recipe for disaster at certain times and in certain places. It is important, of course, to choose a good time and place for working with the subject's creativity. It is also important to prepare the class properly before initiating any activities. A boisterous classroom is almost always going to become even more boisterous when working with creative exercises, whether they be ego- or subject-oriented.

Ego creativity is important when considering the processing of ideas thrown forward by the subject. Schiller claims:

> Regarded in isolation, an idea may be quite insignificant, and venturesome in the extreme, but it may acquire importance from an idea which follows it; perhaps in a certain collection with other ideas, which may seem equally absurd, it may be capable of furnishing a very serviceable link. The intellect cannot judge all these ideas unless it can retain them until it has considered them in connection with these other ideas.
>
> (ibid.)

Hence the ego's capacity to create meaning and set ideas in new contexts comes in handy once the subject's ideas have been allowed to flow forward without the 'watchers at the gates' hindering their progress.

We are now in a position to look more closely at the normal creative activities of the classroom so as to see what the theories developed above might give us in terms of a new understanding and perspective.

Creativity, art and literature: methodological consequences

The conditions (setting the subject's desire and creativity in motion) described above also arise in art (in Lacanian theory everything is structured by the signifier, even pictures, music, sculpture and any other artistic production). The artist will produce paintings for the gaze, the desire of the Other (the art teacher for instance). Without this desire s/he cannot sell (or in some cases even produce) pictures. The eye in Lacanian theory is a cover for object *a*. However, the Other's desire can cause one to 'produce' in the same way that one's own desire can.

> Insofar as the subject is the artist, however, he has already been released from his individual will, and has become, as it were, the medium through which the one truly existent subject, celebrates his release in appearance.
>
> (Nietzsche 2000 [1886]: p. 52)

The relationship between the subject and the object also lies at the heart of sublimation. Freud discussed art in relation to sublimation where the original object of the drive (the object causing frustration) is displaced towards another object (the object of art). Lacan also discusses sublimation. However, the object of the drive is not exchanged for another object, the nature of the object changes. It takes on the position of the 'Thing', intrinsically unknowable. After 1964 the Thing became object *a*, positioning the object in the real. Žižek discussed art as the Thing in *The Fragile Absolute*:

> Another way to make the same point would be to emphasize how in today's art, the gap that separates the sacred space of sublime beauty from the excremental space of trash (leftover) is gradually narrowing, up to the paradoxical identity of opposites are not modern art objects more and more excremental objects, trash (often in a quite literal sense: faeces, rotting corpses) displayed in – made to occupy: to fill in – the sacred place of the thing.
>
> (Žižek 2000: pp. 25–26)

But how is it possible to relate seeing and art to reading and the written word (also important sources of creativity in the classroom)? When discussing seeing and its relation to gesture, which is the foundation of both writing and painting, Lacan claims:

That which in the identificatory dialectic of the signifier and the spoken will be projected forward as haste, is here, on the contrary, the end, that which at the outset of any new intelligence, will be called the moment of seeing. This terminal moment is that which enables us to distinguish between a gesture and an act. It is by means of the gesture that the brushstroke is applied to the canvas. And so true is it that the gesture is always present there that there can be no doubt that the picture is first felt by us, as the terms impression or impressionism imply, as having more affinity with the gesture than with any other type of movement. All action represented in a picture appears to us as a battle scene, that is to say, as something theatrical, necessarily created for the gesture.... What we see here, then is that the gaze operates in a certain descent of desire, no doubt.... The subject is not completely aware of it – he operates by remote control. Modifying the formula I have of desire, as unconscious-man's desire is the desire of the Other – I would say that it is a question of a sort of desire on the part of the Other at the end of which is the 'showing' (le donner-à-voir). How could this showing satisfy something, if there is not some appetite of the eye on the part of the person looking? This appetite of the eye produces the hypnotic value of painting.

(Lacan 1964: pp. 114–115)

There is an opening of the floodgates then (to use Schiller's words), a small moment of madness (a battle scene) when the subject pushes through and takes over (as by remote control). The eye covers object *a*, according to Lacan in *Seminar X*. Thus the subject will be driven by the Other's desire and the subject's desire will move around object *a*. It sees me, I see it seeing me, etc. The relationship between the gesture and the act is likened here to the relationship between the signifier and the spoken word: 'The identificatory dialectic of the signifier and the spoken will be projected forward as haste .. the moment of seeing .. enables us to distinguish between a gesture and an act' (ibid). As in painting, writing is produced by the gesture,

> The poet makes himself a seer by a long, gigantic and rational derangement of all the senses ... he becomes among all men ... the supreme Scholar! ... Because he reaches the unknown.
>
> (Rimbaud 2005 [1871]: p. 377)

while reading is produced by the act of seeing. This might explain the production of texts and paintings by the subject, but what creative processes take place when reading or listening to a text?

In a text there must be rupture or natural breaks which don't elicit the ego of the reader. There are plenty of texts spoken and written which are directed towards the ego of the reader or listener. In fact most texts are. So let us look at the specific ruptures in Lacan's texts that are not directed towards the ego. In considering Lacan's narrative, there are a variety of techniques to create the dream-like quality of his texts. Amongst other things, Lacan uses double negation to disconnect the ego and create a state of mind that allows the reader to experience a sense of something being 'beyond' the text but within reach, causing the mind to work hard, trying to reach that 'beyond'. Double negation is an old technique; Shakespeare used it in his texts. Double negation can also be used interchangeably with 'impossible statements' such as 'listen to the sound of one hand clapping' (Zen Buddhists have used these for meditation for centuries). Lacan liked playing with words and presenting the reader with riddles. He also used humour, incomplete sentences or unanswered questions, leaving the reader to fill in the gaps and answer the unanswered. I will give a few examples here of the techniques mentioned above. In *The Four Fundamental Concepts of Psychoanalysis*, Lacan claims:

> The ancients recognized all kinds of things in dreams, including on occasion, messages from the gods – and why not? The ancients made something of these messages from the gods. And, anyway – perhaps you will glimpse this in what I shall say later – who knows, the gods may still speak through dreams. Personally, I don't mind either way. What concerns us is the tissue that envelops these messages, the network in which, on occasion something is caught. Perhaps the voice of the gods makes itself heard, but it is a long time since men lent their ears to them in their original state – it is well known that the ears are made not to hear with.
>
> (Lacan 1964: p. 45)

The last sentence is a typical nonsensical statement. When creating riddles Lacan borrowed from modern art (which he collected quite extensively). In discussing the drive, for instance, Lacan claimed that it was very similar to a montage, thus allowing him to create his own modernistic picture (in many ways reminiscent of a Dali painting):

> The montage of the drive is a montage which, first, is presented as having neither head nor tail – in the sense in which one speaks of montage in a surrealist collage. If we bring together the paradoxes that we just defined at the level of Drang, at that of the object, at that of the aim of the drive, I think that the resulting image would show the working of a dynamo connected to the gas-tap, a peacock's feather emerges, and tickles the belly of a pretty woman, who is just lying there looking beautiful. Indeed, the thing begins to become more interesting from this very fact, that the drive defines, according to Freud, all the forms of which one may reverse such a mechanism. This does not mean that one turns the dynamo upside-down – one unrolls its wires,

it is they that become the peacock's feather, the gas-tap goes onto the lady's mouth, and the bird's rump emerges in the middle.

(ibid.: p. 169)

When the text is ruptured by one of the 'methods' discussed above, Bergstedt (1998) argues a gap opens up, bringing the creativity of the subject into play. This is often consciously experienced by the reader as a change in awareness, leading to new insights which come suddenly, or 'out of the blue'. Texts allowing for such an 'opening up' towards the unconscious often result in a deep sense of change in the reader. Most of us have had such experiences. We don't always know why one book touched us more than others, but we do not deny the difference in depth or dignity. Double negations and riddles are not the only techniques for creating ruptures or gaps in a text; metaphor or a change in rhetorical style can also create rupture.

What consequences might the Lacanian theory discussed above have for the understanding of creativity in the classroom? When considering the current chapter we can conclude that there are two forms of creativity, that of the subject and that of the ego. The creativity of the subject can best be understood in relation to dreams. However, eliciting the subject's speech relies on processes more akin to those seen in therapy – which is not to say that subject creativity results in any deep delving into the students' minds. Rather it points to possible methodologies such as using riddles, mysteries and the like so as to set the subject's creativity in motion. It also points to the relationship created between the teacher and the student. Here the teacher positions him/herself as the subject-supposed-to-know (the specialist who has knowledge which is not easily available to the student) or, alternatively, the Other who sees his/her students and expects them to achieve. This sets the subject's desire in motion, the desire to know what the teacher knows, or the desire to achieve as the teacher expects the subject to achieve, which is hopefully present in all classrooms. The ego's censorious response should be avoided when eliciting the subject's creativity and therefore any classroom exercise involving both should probably start with the creativity of the subject and move on to the creativity of the ego, as the former provides material for the latter.

Art classes which involve painting and sculpture, as well as classes which involve creative writing, will probably quite inadvertently elicit the creativity of the subject as long as the student isn't beset by rules and regulations as to how and what should be produced.

There are of course other ways to set our students' creative subjects in motion, as has been suggested above. Some teachers create a mystery to be solved, which at times can be as popular as the bookstores' top-ten best-selling detective stories. Sessions with riddles, games and problems to be solved, interspersed with humour, will also set the subject in motion. These riddles should not have an obvious or necessarily meaningful solution, as this would stimulate the creativity of the ego rather than that of the subject. Lacanian texts are a good example of how such riddles and mysteries can be set up. It is important to inform the students of the aim of the riddles and mysteries, i.e. creative thought. Otherwise they will react with frustration and anger, which is often the case when the ego is confronted by something it does not understand and feels it should – students should of course feel challenged, not stupid.

Sadly Lacanian texts have elicited a great deal of irritation when approached without the knowledge that they are written to elicit both the creative thought of the subject and the ego. Lacanian theorists have at times been seen as belonging to an elitist club for philosophers and psychoanalysts engaged in intellectual gymnastics with terminology so dense and complicated that it excludes a large part of the academic community. This in turn has led to very angry reactions from those suspecting Lacanian terminology of being a case of 'Emperor's new clothes'. It is true that to go deeply into Lacanian theory demands a confrontation with both philosophical texts and psychoanalytic texts. However, this is not necessary for those who wish to use Lacanian texts as a creative tool. Parveen recommended that anybody reading Lacanian texts concentrated directly on these instead of attempting to read all the philosophical forerunners to the texts. In other words, it is enough to read the texts, it is not necessary to understand them in their entirety, as this is neither possible nor desirable, especially where Lacan is concerned.

Summary

We can observe the subject's thoughts in dreams. The subject is a story teller, creating scripts as well as casting the roles and creating the stage backdrops for each evening's plays. It is an intelligent and lucid story teller, cloaking the dreamer's desire behind a variety of personas, which in turn demands the perseverance of a sleuth to untangle and analyse the hidden meaning of the drama (or everyday scenario) which unfolds. This great wealth of creativity exists within each individual. It is a dimension of our personas over which we have little control but every possibility to make use of as both teachers and students. Artists such as Schiller learnt to channel the creativity of the story teller for their own purposes. Freud used it to access repressed memories which he believed would provide him with a key to his patient's health. As teachers this source of creativity is yet to be used in any systematic way. However, we do so inadvertently when we use classroom exercises which involve free association.

Free association was used originally in Freudian therapy. Freud likens this to the flow of creativity mentioned by Schiller in his letter to Körner. Further, he claimed that neither he nor his patients had any problems in achieving the state of mind necessary to reach this dimension of creativity (or consciousness). On the other hand, Freudian analysis was never straightforward. The subject's thoughts often show themselves through gaps, ruptures and 'the half-said' (according to Lacan), which demands a great deal from the interpreter or analyst. Even when the subject's speech is lucid and seemingly meaningful, it is often non-contextual and non-sequential. Interpretation of the subject's speech has much in common with the interpretation of poetry. Many poets can't interpret their own work and leave it up to the reader. Lacan claims the subject does not wish to mislead us and therefore our attempts are likely to be rewarded.

The subject's creativity is set in motion when faced with the Other's desire (I will discuss this at greater length in the next chapter). Here the teacher's unconscious desire (desire for object *a*) drives the students' creativity. Being caught by the Other's desire is related to the gaze (the experience of being seen or having been seen). The gaze also drives the creativity of artists and writers.

The ego processes the ideas brought by the subject, i.e. *connaissance* and *savoir*. Both interact in creative endeavour. Painting, writing and reading can all be an expression of the subject's creativity. The first two are a response to the gaze, and the second to ruptures and gaps in the text. Double negations, riddles and mysteries can be used to set the subjects creativity in motion, over and above ruptures, gaps, the gaze and the Other's desire (the subject speaks when the ego is in doubt, according to Lacan).

In Chapters 1 and 2 I introduced a variety of theoretical concepts which have been developed further through this chapter, such as the subject, *jouissance*, desire, object *a*, the Other, *connaissance* and *savoir*. These concepts will be expanded upon in the next chapter. There are, however, several questions that arise in relation to what has been presented here. What, for instance, does Lacan actually mean when he claims that the gaze can act as a cover for object *a*?

We know the object is imaginary (i.e. we can cover our lack with a variety of imaginary objects), which is partially why we continue to desire what others desire, believing their conscious desire might hold the solution to our own. This results in conformity, desire for the same luxury goods, the same 'life style' requirements, etc. Lacan originally claimed that imaginary 'part' objects can cover object *a*, such as the breast, the phallus, the gaze, the voice, the faeces and the urinal flow. These objects cannot be properly assimilated into the mirror image of the body, the ideal. They do not belong to the vision of mastery (belonging to the ideal) and cannot be fully controlled as, for instance, in bedwetting, being seen to do something wrong, say something wrong or being told something is wrong, something which is 'not in line' with the ideal. Part objects 'hang loose' and can free themselves and cause the child and adult anxiety, such as a flashback of an early memory of enuresis or an embarrassing moment when we were discovered doing something socially unacceptable. They are, in other words, a part of social anxiety and social expectations. Hence the gaze can drive the artist in his or her wishes to 'perform' the socially acceptable act of producing great art.

The gaze of the Other can also act as a cover for object *a* in the real, i.e. as a representative of the *jouissance* lost during the Oedipus Complex.

> I would say that it is a question of a sort of desire on the part of the Other at the end of which is the 'showing' (le donner-à-voir). How could this showing satisfy something, if there is not some appetite of the eye on the part of the person looking?
>
> (Lacan 1998 [1964]: pp. 114–115)

In the quote above, the voracious appetite of the eye demands a 'showing'. This can be a perverse gaze (the hungry eye never gets enough) which drives performance, fuelled by the aggressive side of the superego. A superego which demands 'enjoy!' (filled with *jouissance* which has returned from the real, 'evil *jouissance*', causing anxiety and driving desire) and is involved in both scoptophilia and sadism (just how bad scoptophilia can get is portrayed in the film *Peeping Tom*). The gaze can, however, also belong to the teacher who has taken the position of object *a* (as in Parveen's lecture). This 'positioning' belongs to the discourse of the analyst, as we shall see in the next chapter. The analyst's discourse is one of four discourses.

Connaissance, and *savoir* are necessary for creative endeavour. These dimensions of knowledge belong to the orders of the imaginary (*connaissance*) and the symbolic (*savoir*). Knowledge and creativity developed in the student–teacher relationship is related to desire, object *a* and *jouissance*, according to Lacan. While this chapter has focused on describing the relationship between the subject of the symbolic and creativity, arguing that creativity in Parveen's classroom was primarily produced by the subject, my next chapter will focus on the interrelation between *connaissance*, *savoir* and *savoir-faire*. In other words, the relationship between primary and secondary processes within the creative endeavour. Further, it will describe how the teacher–student relationship can help us understand this process in a variety of educational settings. These do not (surprisingly) produce the same relationship to creativity, knowledge and *jouissance*, as we shall see. Lacan's four discourses will also allow us to investigate the relation of power between students and teachers, and how this affects the production of knowledge and creativity in the classroom. The discourses were presented during the student riots in Paris in 1969, which had consequences for how Lacan visualised teacher–student relations within the university.

Finally, I would like to add that a creative classroom is almost always a classroom of laughter and fun. The work is as serious as any other. Playing games is not the same as 'game playing'. All too often teachers believe that riddles, games, mysteries and other similar techniques are simply a way of giving the students a break, and are not representative of serious work. But if creativity is the aim, it is precisely these kinds of techniques which will give results. Lacanian theory also shows that we should not be fearful of presenting difficult theories or enigmatic texts, as long as the student understands that it is done with the aim to set his/her creativity in motion. In an attempt to be faithful to this argument, the next chapter will partially be enigmatic, and represents a steep progression on the path to which I have subscribed. There will be symbolic formulae to contend with, and a variety of discourses and schedules to which these are applied. There will also be sections supplying rather pragmatic explanations (describing easily recognised classroom situations). However, primarily the next chapter should be considered, in part, an application of the theory of creativity and methodologies discussed above.

Chapter 4

Knowledge, creativity and the four discourses

Introduction

Knowledge is a means to pleasure or *jouissance* according to Lacan. In this chapter I will investigate the relationship between knowledge, *jouissance* and creativity. Further, I will attempt to discover more about the interplay between

'Where your treasure is, there will your heart be also', our treasure is where the beehives of our knowledge are. We are constantly making for them, being by nature winged creatures and honeygatherers of the spirit; there is one thing alone we really care about from the heart – 'bringing something home'.

(Nietzsche 2000 [1887]: p. 451)

conscious and unconscious knowledge. To do so I will discuss Lacan's four discourses: the Master's discourse, the Hysteric's discourse, the University discourse and the Analyst's discourse (Lacan 1969–1970, 1972–1973). In these Lacan's pedagogic oeuvre is mapped out in the shape of four mathematical formulae along with two schedules. The latter are meant to be superimposed over the former to expand their explanatory capacity. The mathematical formulae are a typical example of Lacan's creative methodologies. However, as these normally appeal only to those well versed in mathematics (and can be experienced as quite off-putting by those who are not) I shall proceed to discuss their contents before introducing them in symbolic form.

The four formulas

The formulas can be applied to a variety of educational settings and describe the relationship between the agent of the discourse (here the teacher/lecturer) and the other (student). Lacan discusses Socrates' pedagogy in *Menon* when illustrating the relationship between the teacher and the student in the discourse of the master, which is the foundation of all other discourses. This discourse has its origins in Kojeve's interpretation of Hegel's *Phenomenology*. The relationship described here is that of the master and the slave. The other discourses are derived from the Master's discourse by turning this discourse clockwise. In the University discourse the relationship between the professor and the PhD student is discussed. The Analyst's discourse is best illustrated by the discussions in the previous chapter, where Parveen's lessons were taken as an example. The Hysteric's discourse is similar, the difference being that students produce knowledge to please their teacher and not as a response to riddles or mysteries to be solved. Further, the teacher does not attempt to interpret this knowledge.

Lacan has (as I discussed previously) a rather complicated relationship to knowledge. On the one hand, all conscious knowledge is imaginary (*connaissance*), on the other hand, unconscious knowledge produced by the subject (*savoir*) is analysed, understood and eventually integrated into the ego's conscious knowledge during therapy, changing the way the analysand perceives him/herself and/or interacts with his/her surroundings. These orders are, amongst other things, related to implicit and explicit memory, which in turn is the foundation of explicit knowledge and so-called implicit knowledge discussed within pedagogy. The relationship between the agent and the other plays out on both a conscious and unconscious level, as does the production of 'knowledge' which the discourses describe. This is not as complicated as it sounds. This relationship circles around desire. In most of the discourses the teacher is placed in the position of desire. Indeed, the teacher is driven by a desire for knowledge or, alternatively, a desire to be desired, according to Lacan. Let us first take a closer look at the discourses and how these might be applied to a classroom setting so as to better understand Lacan's pedagogical theory (involving knowledge and creativity) before moving on to discuss what they might enable in terms of an understanding of *jouissance* and creativity.

4 × 4

The discourses, as I claimed earlier, are described in four formulas. Each formula has four positions. The agent, in the top left-hand corner, is separated from the bottom left-hand corner by a bar under which the position of truth appears. The other, in the top right-hand of the formula, is separated by a bar from the bottom right-hand position, where production appears. There are four factors which come into play in the discourses. One is the divided subject ($); one is the object (a); the third is the primary signifier (S1), which can either represent the half-truths spoken during analysis or the law; and the fourth is the secondary signifier (S2), which can either be seen as a collection of signifiers or as *le savoir* (knowledge). The discourses describe a relationship between the agent (of the discourse) and the other (recipient of the discourse). The agent is active and attempts to make the 'other' productive; the other responds to this in a variety of ways depending on the discourse. Further, the agent covers the truth of his/her condition by presenting a façade to the other. The agent may, for instance, in truth be divided ($), but will present him/herself as the law (S1) in the Master's discourse or as knowledge (S2) in the University discourse when s/he is, in truth, driven by the law (S1).

The Master's and the Hysteric's discourse: excellence and desire

In the Master's discourse the relationship described is that of the master and the slave. The master takes the position of the agent and presents him/herself as the law (S1). However, s/he is hiding the truth. The truth is that the master is lacking and divided ($). This lack or division causes the master to desire but to not know what s/he desires. The master sets the slave to work. The slave is in the position of the other. S/he has 'know-how' or *savoir faire* (S2), which is a type of bodily knowledge

SOCRATES: Tell me now, boy, you know that a square figure is like this? – I do.

SOCRATES: A square then is a figure in which all these four sides are equal? – Yes indeed.

SOCRATES: And it also has these lines through the middle equal? – Yes....

SOCRATES: What do you think, Meno? Has he, in his answers, expressed any opinion that was not his own.

MENO: No they are all his own.

SOCRATES: So these opinions were in him, were they not? – Yes.

SOCRATES: So the man who does not know has within himself true opinions about the things that he does not know? – So it appears....

SOCRATES: If he has not acquired them in his present life, is it not clear that he had them and had learned them at some other time? – It seems so.

(Plato 1997 [380 BC]: pp. 881–886)

that has not been consciously realised in so far that the other cannot express his/her knowledge in terms of theory. However, the slave has knowledge (on an unconscious level) and produces what the master desires. In fact, the slave produces it in surplus (object *a*), but as the master does not know what s/he desires, the object will never be recognised and so the master simply demands more and more work which leads to surplus. The discourse describes the classical relationship between the capitalist and the labourer, the constant production leading to surplus, or object *a*.

$$\frac{S1}{\$} \rightarrow \frac{S2}{a}$$

When discussing the Master's discourse Lacan refers to Socrates. In *Menon* he questions a slave boy as to the area of a square. The boy claims to have no prior knowledge, but prompted by Socrates' questions produces the correct 'knowledge'. Knowledge Socrates then uses (disinheriting the slave) as proof of his own theory, i.e. that knowledge is inherent to each individual.

The Master's discourse: theories of excellence

Translated into an educational setting we might position the teacher in place of the agent and the student in the position of the other. Here the lecturer/teacher will put the student to work as this is expected in an institutional setting. Further, the lecturer/teacher is in a position of power and has the right to exercise the law. The law demands that the students should follow institutional regulations, carry out homework and sit institutional exams. They have knowledge and are required to prove this by producing documents which can be graded and marked. The student is required to pass these exams and to learn. However, there is always something outside or beyond institutional laws and regulations (object *a*) and it is this object the lecturer/teacher desires. But what might this object be?

We know that teachers/lecturers desire students to produce knowledge, which is achieved within the educational setting, so object *a* must be something else. Let us test the hypothesis that object *a* is 'excellence'. The conditions for excellence can be quite elusive (which fits our purposes). Excellence is always achieved somewhere else, in other institutions, schools or universities, and with other students. The students, on the other hand, may know what the lecturer wants and produce it. They may even be given the highest grades for doing so. However (according to the discourse) the lecturer/teacher will still suffer from a sense of dissatisfaction. S/he will not understand what the object of his/her desire is, even when confronted by it.

It follows that this lecturer/teacher would probably be happiest during term time when students are producing plenty of work, as this work might eventually result in excellence. At the end of the year when grades are set the teacher/lecturer may be left with a sense of anticlimax, possibly even emptiness which continues even if s/he wins awards, general recognition from the principal and/or other staff. Holidays may be spent planning for the next term and wondering what might be done to eventually reach the elusive state of excellence.

Further, this lecturer may be very sensitive to criticism as s/he is covering a divided (faulty) subject with the law (a rather defensive position to start with). All subjects are divided because of the Oedipus Complex (no matter what appears in the position of truth in the discourses), but all agents/teachers do not take the position of master or law. Criticism from colleagues or students could be more severely considered and deeply felt than anybody suspects and when less gracefully received could even lead to long-held grudges or, at worst, a need for retribution. There are many students who have experienced cold dislike from a teacher/lecturer who cannot bear to be criticised or shown up. Outwardly the lecturer could appear to be confident. S/he might even be a trailblazer with enormous amounts of energy, whipping students up and on towards more and more achievements (e.g. gym teachers and trainers); s/he could also be an author-itarian (Hyldgaard 2008), running 'a tight ship' and placing great emphasis on being fair, meting out rewards for good achievements; or a calm, kind – almost paternal/maternal – lecturer, but under the surface many master teachers/lecturers demand absolute loyalty and good work, responding with disappointment to failure and questioning of his/her authority or judgement (Lacan was often perceived to be a 'stern father' during the student uprising).

The master lecturer/teacher is likely to be seen by some students as the one who continues to demand far beyond what is felt to be viable or acceptable, constantly citing rules and regulations. By others this demand is seen as what in and of itself creates results. These students often claim that no work would be produced at all if the lecturer was not 'in charge'. There are students who feel secure in a learning environment where the lecturer or teacher is a master and where rules are made to be followed and grades are given according to production scales. Later in life, at class reunions for example, the master lecturer is often described as 'not too bad really'. Others might claim that they learnt more during the master lecturer's lessons than any other, though s/he wasn't liked very much, etc. However, some will blame their aversion to all kinds of education on the rigid rules and 'blind demands' of the master lecturer's classroom.

The Hysteric's discourse: the object of desire

The second discourse is that of the hysteric. The hysteric is the (agent) of the discourse and is in fact (in the position of truth) object a. However, the hysteric refuses to be recognised as the object and presents him/herself as lacking ($), divided and/or undesirable.

I am the scholar in his dark armchair. Branches and rain beat against the library window.

I am the wanderer along the main road running through the dwarfish woods. The noise of the sluices drowns my footsteps. For a long time I can see the sad golden wash of the sunset.

I might be the child abandoned on the wharf setting out for the high seas, or the farmland, following the path whose top reaches the sky.

(Rimbaud 2005 [1872–1974?]: p. 313)

The therapist is in the position of the other and attempts to lay down the law (S1), and in so doing tries to help the hysteric position him/herself in relation to the law so as to find an answer to the riddle 'what is it to be a man?' or 'what is it to be a woman?' (this is the main question driving the hysteric). However, the hysteric is not satisfied. In response to every question s/he poses, answered one way or another by the therapist, the hysteric will shake his/her head, 'that's not it'. The therapist strains in his/her attempt to position the law and help the hysteric, and thereby produces knowledge (S2). 'What matters to her is that the other called a man knows what a precious object she (the hysteric) becomes in this context of discourse' (Lacan 2007 [1969–1970]: p. 34). The hysteric attempts to incite the therapist's desire to know her/him. Lacan claims: 'We therefore see the hysteric fabricate a man as best she can – a man who would be animated by the desire to know' (ibid.: p. 34). 'The desire to know is not what leads to knowledge. What leads to knowledge is [...] the hysteric's discourse' (ibid.: p. 23).

$$\frac{\$}{a} \rightarrow \frac{S1}{S2}$$

The lecturer/teacher with a hysteric's discourse presents him/herself as lacking, somebody searching for knowledge, knowledge s/he does not have. Further, this lecturer behaves as if the students hold the answer; they have the elusive knowledge s/he is looking for (S1) – i.e. knowledge of the subject – and in so doing causes the students to produce knowledge (S2). This lecturer might be found together with his/her students reminiscing about jungle trekking in Guatemala, visits with Buddhist monks in Nepal, two-month lorry treks through northern Africa, searching for some kind of answer. His/her stories will mesmerise the students and therefore this lecturer will often be popular. The lecturer who takes the position of the hysteric will often down play his/her own status or position – s/he might even claim that s/he doesn't have as much knowledge as the students believe, or that prior knowledge is unimportant. Rather it is the process leading up to knowledge, the creative process that is important. However, it is not knowledge this lecturer desires, it is rather the student–lecturer relationship which is central, coupled with a wish to be desired.

This lecturer creates seductive questions. Questions which will make the students feel that they already have the answers. S/he might even allow the students to structure their own search for knowledge, as well as design their own classroom conditions and regulations (S1). Empowered with new authority, incited by an enigmatic teacher/lecturer they will happily produce knowledge. Every time they attempt to present knowledge or a solution to a problem, the lecturer will listen with interest and admiration, but just as the argument seems to be wrapped up s/he will hesitate and add 'It's good but could there be something else?', or 'Is there, for instance, a different way of looking at the problem?' The teacher is an enigma, a mystery waiting to be solved. What is s/he lacking? What is s/he searching for? What answer does s/he want? S/he will set in motion the desire for knowledge. It is for her/him that the students produce, not because s/he demands it, but because s/he is in the position of truth, the object of desire.

There are, however, students uncomfortable with all the uncertainties produced. In some cases students become frustrated because they suspect the lecturer has the holy grail of knowledge (s/he is object *a*) but is refusing to share it, making the whole learning situation unnecessarily complicated.

A feeling arises which might be summed up by the expression 'Just get on with it', or 'Who do you think you are kidding?'. They sense there is a masquerade going on! A ruse!

The University and the Analyst's discourse: more is less

An anti-clockwise turn of the Master's discourse produces the University discourse (which is also the discourse of science). Here the position of truth is taken by (S1), the law. The law demands 'continue to learn' and is covered or represented by knowledge (S2). The position of the slave in the Master's discourse is now taken by the student, or the '*a* student' as Lacan claims. The students are object *a*. They are the guarantors of knowledge or, as Lacan claims, 'are requested to constitute the subject of science with their own skins' (Lacan 2007 [1969–1970]: pp. 105–106). They must produce, but their production results in the divided subject ($). The more they produce the more divided they become. Knowledge simply leads to the production/ realisation of lack. We cannot know everything however hard we try.

$$\frac{S2}{S1} \rightarrow \frac{a}{\$}$$

The University discourse: amassing knowledge and getting less

The lecturer/teacher of the University discourse is knowledgeable. S/he knows, seems indeed to be all-knowing (S2). S/he is driven by the law (S1), which demands and forces him/her to learn more and more. S/he in turn will demand that the stu-

> I intend to unveil all mysteries: religious mysteries or those of nature, death, birth, the future, the past, cosmogony, the void.... I possess every talent! – There is no one here and there is someone. I would not like to expend my treasure.
>
> (Rimbaud 2005 [1873]: p. 277)

dents become the guarantee for object *a* (they are object *a*). Their research is knowledge (the university could not exist without students producing doctoral theses). However, the more the students produce the more divided they become. The result is lack. The lecturer will be satisfied but the students less so – they learn the ultimate truth of division. They will never be whole. Knowledge will never be complete. There is never enough. The lecturer does not care for this piece of information – s/he keeps setting new students to work. Knowledge is 'king' and s/he intends to have as much of it as possible. S/he is forever reading, learning and writing new articles (if s/he has time to take a break from amassing new knowledge!). S/he will be recognised as the specialist, the one who knows as this is how s/he presents him/herself. S/he is the boffin but s/he looks to the students for new interesting answers to research problems. 'Go forth and multiply' is his/her command.

The Analyst's discourse: wanting to know what the Other knows

A quarter-turn clockwise of the Hysteric's discourse produces the Analyst's discourse. In this discourse the analyst presents him/herself as the object of desire (object *a*), but is in truth (the position of truth) the holder of knowledge (S2). S/he has to present him/herself as object *a* to set the analysand's desire in motion. The analysand occupies the position of the slave and comes to the therapy aware that s/he is lacking something ($). During analysis the desire for the therapist causes him/her to produce (S1) the master signifier, which in therapy relates to half-truths from which the therapist creates knowledge. The therapist is forcing forth true speech from the subject. In here lies fragments of the law, of the fundamental fantasy and of many other symbolic aspects in the analysand's unconscious. These fragments seem at first disjointed and enigmatic. The therapist works to make sense of them and in so doing creates knowledge.

> I am working to make myself a Seer.... It is a question of reaching the unknown.... It is wrong to say I think: One ought to say: people think me.... I is someone else.
>
> (Rimbaud 2005 [1871]: p. 371)

$$\frac{a}{S2} \rightarrow \frac{\$}{S1}$$

The lecturer/teacher who has an Analyst's discourse will present him/herself as 'the one who knows'. S/he not only has knowledge, but *is* knowledge. This teacher/lecturer is highly respected, revered and even feared, causing students to feel intensely aware of their own lack of knowledge. They will look to the lecturer to enlighten them. Confusion often arises when the demand for knowledge issues forth from this lecturer. It might come in the shape of a mystery to be solved or a riddle. The teacher will say that there are no stupid answers, students should not be shy with their response. At first the students will strain to produce an answer. When this turns out to be unsuccessful, students might produce answers (any answer) in pure exasperation. Here they enter into the game of free association and their subjects start to create knowledge. From these answers the teacher will extract the 'truth', knowledge which will be given content by the teacher who will show the students how and why they have produced something valuable.

This lecturer/teacher risks frustrating his students. However, when the production of S1 has started the students will feel elated and creative. Their creativity will be recognised and in this they develop and grow. The biggest risk is the loss of students before their creativity is released. The lecturer/teacher will demand that students tuck away their egos and empty their cups of knowledge so that they might be filled again, but this time from within. Competition is not recommended – rather contemplation and meditation aided by philosophy and art. Cooperation, understanding and acceptance are key words.

This discourse is the one I experienced in Parveen's classroom. We produced and she rapidly set our odd creations into a meaningful context. The analyst lecturer is often considered to 'see' his/her students, to understand the depths of his/her proselytes, to call up their hidden capacities and make them grow. The process can, of course, also be painful and annoying, making students aware of their shortcomings.

Jouissance and creativity in the Analyst's and Master's discourses

Knowledge is a means to pleasure or *jouissance* according to Lacan. The elation experienced by students in the analyst's discourse is caused by the production of signifiers to which *jouissance* is attached. How might

> Again for the pleasure and delight of knowledge, and learning, it far surpasseth all other in nature: ... there is no satiety, but satisfaction and appetite are perpetually interchangeable.
>
> (Bacon 2002 [1605]: p. 167)

we understand this 'odd' alliance between *jouissance* and the signifier.

The hysteric's symptom is mediated through the sign which is pleasurable when considering secondary gains. Further, tattoos and scarification are signs on the skin which result in *jouissance* according to Lacan.

Jouissance *and the Signifier: Llalangue*

In *Seminar XX* Lacan claims that Llalangue, which underpins all language, is permeated by *jouissance*. Llalangue can perhaps best be seen

> I invented the colour of the vowels.... I regulated the form and movement of each consonant ... in my alchemy of the word
>
> (Rimbaud 2005 [1873]: p. 285)

in relation to children's play with words and rhyme (they play with signifiers which make up language). This form of pleasure is different from pleasure experienced during mastery. The latter belongs to the ego, which aims to understand and control. However, the subject's knowledge will eventually be integrated by the ego, and at that point both forms of pleasure interplay. In 'creativity research' the subject's knowledge is often claimed to be a part of 'primary processes' and the ego's of secondary. Primary processes are considered to be working away 'on the quiet', while secondary processes are those that develop after 'disguised material' from the unconscious has emerged to cause the famous 'aha experience'. There is a difference between traditional theories explaining the 'aha experience' and the theory presented here. The subject's speech in Lacanian theory is not an expression of a repressed unconscious which, working away on the quiet, produces creative knowledge, later (at the right moment) voiced in the classroom. On the contrary, the subject speaks, carrying out its creative work for all to hear and see. Further, the experience is often developed through social interaction. This 'other' or 'Other' might be physically present or only present as an internalised gaze. Just like the painter might produce a painting for a specific buyer, the student might be producing knowledge in response to a parent, a friend or another teacher.

How are *jouissance* and creativity positioned in the other discourses described here? If positioned at all?

The Master's discourse: obtaining pleasure but little else

Let us first turn to the Master's discourse (frequently observed in educational institutions). The student has knowledge in terms of *savoir-faire* (know-how), which is more akin to physical knowledge owing to age and experience. They know how to produce knowledge demanded by the

> We are eager to see, and learn things. We reckon that the acquisition of knowledge of hidden or remarkable features is necessary for the happy life.... Associated with this eagerness for the vision of the truth is a kind of aspiration for leadership, so that the mind well fashioned by nature is willing to obey only a moral guide or teacher or commander who issues just and lawful orders for our benefit.
>
> (Cicero 2008 [44 BC]: p. 7)

teacher. As knowledge is a means to *jouissance*, we might safely assume that the student has some of it, although being attached to production it will be appropriated by the teacher soon enough. The student's work will be refined and forged into theoretical knowledge by the teacher as proof that his/her students are progressing as expected. The teacher is more firmly immersed in the symbolic order as s/he is schooled in theory and directed to set the student's knowledge and progress into theoretical frameworks or into charts of expected norms of performance. This act of appropriation places *jouissance* (excess *jouissance*) on the side of the teacher or master.

Lacan explains the relationship of appropriation and loss in two different schedules which can be superimposed over the discourses described above and used to analyse these. The master signifier is placed in the upper left-hand corner of the first schedule. The master signifier is the agent and therefore has a position of power in the discourse. Knowledge is positioned in the top right-hand corner. *Jouissance* (excess) is positioned beneath the bar in the lower right-hand corner. This is the product of the student which the teacher later appropriates. The subject of the unconscious is positioned in the bottom left-hand corner, under the master signifier.

$$\frac{\text{Master signifier}}{\text{Subject}} \rightarrow \frac{\text{Knowledge}}{\textit{Jouissance}}$$

In the second schedule desire is positioned in the top left-hand corner, over the position of truth. The Other is positioned in the top right-hand corner. Depicting both a place and a person, the Other is the 'unconscious' of the recipient (the student). Loss is positioned under the bar in the bottom right-hand corner.

$$\frac{\text{Desire}}{\text{Truth}} \rightarrow \frac{\text{Other}}{\text{Loss}}$$

This enables Lacan to argue that the student's knowledge is not fully articulated or fully conscious. The student knows what to do to produce the knowledge desired by the teacher, but does not necessarily know how to understand this knowledge theoretically, or how to cloak it in theoretical terms. This knowledge leads to *jouissance*. However, it will be appropriated by the teacher (a process depicted by loss). The students must work, and work is not necessarily related to *jouissance*.

This discourse mainly points to pleasure generated by the ego's mastery. Students will experience pleasure during the production of knowledge and its integration by the ego. There is a sense of achievement and satisfaction. Good exam results can even lead to elation. While every master/teacher must work to appropriate knowledge concerning their students' progress (via the students' own production of knowledge), pleasure felt when the last term papers have been graded and most students passed the course requirements can be quite substantial. But what of creativity in the Master's discourse?

The student produces knowledge at the level of the Other. This knowledge is unconscious knowledge. Having *savoir-faire* or 'know-how' relates to producing knowledge as expected by the master. What is at stake here is reproductive knowledge, for although *jouissance* and unconscious knowledge is involved, the master does not recognise this knowledge. The master wants what the student has but doesn't know what this is as desire of the other's desire is unconscious. Hence any creative knowledge that emerges does not get interpreted or understood by the student or the master. This is not a discourse where free association suffices or passes as knowledge which can be graded (normally). Reproductive knowledge is, however, important and serves to prove that the student has understood something. This type of knowledge will often be taken by the master and set into a theoretical framework which can then be given back to the student in terms of an explanation or grades. The student's *savoir-faire* is thus used to illustrate something the teacher knows the student must learn, as for instance in the case of Socrates and Meno. But the master, at the heart of his/her desire, is actually looking for the elusive knowledge produced by the unconscious, but cannot recognise it and will feel the lack. Excellence, as I claimed earlier, is always somewhere else.

The Master's discourse is not a creative discourse and much of creativity research points to the lack of interest in creativity in schools where productivity and the capacity to reproduce is held at a premium.

Desire for knowledge, desire for the lecturer: the University and Hysteric's discourses

The University discourse fairs no better under the Lacanian magnifying glass. *Jouissance* is firmly placed on the side of the lecturer, who is driven by his/her desire for knowledge, powered on to be all-knowing by the superego's command that s/he must learn more.

The University discourse: signifiers to feed the lecturer

In the University discourse the PhD students are simply the guarantee for knowledge (object *a*), albeit unconsciously. Consciously they will become more and more aware that they are lacking. That there is no way of making a PhD thesis complete or whole and that their knowledge will never be enough. It is hard to see how *jouissance* might arrive on the side of the PhD student. However, s/he is

... for whereas the more constant devoted kind of professors of any science ought to propound to themselves to make some additions to their science, they convert their labours to aspire to certain second prizes.... For men have entered into a desire of learning and knowledge, sometimes upon a natural curiosity and inquisitive appetite; sometimes to entertain their minds with variety and delight; sometimes for ornament and reputation; and sometimes to enable them to victory of wit and contradiction; and most times for lucre and profession....

(Bacon 2002: p. 147)

also amassing knowledge and as knowledge is always a means to *jouissance* on the side of the unconscious and pleasure on the side of the conscious, the student must also have acquired a fair share of both. In positioning the barred/divided subject in the place of loss, Lacan is emphasising that this *jouissance* will, however, be drained from the student (even if pleasure will be present on completion of the thesis). Going through the process of taking a PhD is a rite of passage where the student will lose his/her 'innocence'. This innocence relates to the belief that complete knowledge could exist anywhere in the world or that the PhD might represent the missing piece, making the student feel whole again. The lecturer has discovered this 'truth' a long time ago and is instead immersed in the game of the university. This game is acquisition and accumulation, and the lecturer is well ahead of the competition, placing his/her name on as many research papers as possible, counting publications and using his/her PhD students to further the game strategies. Pleasure here lies in amassing knowledge, of positively filling oneself with signifiers. The student represents (in the position of the Other) a swarm of new signifiers on which to feast. Is creativity necessary for this discourse? Surprisingly not!

Most people believe the university to be a creative place, but like the Master's discourse, reproduction is of the essence. It is a part of the university's strategy to prove that it is producing something 'real'. If many people produce and reproduce the same results over time then these must be 'safe' or correct. Over and above reproduction, repetition is essential otherwise scientific research would collapse. All experiments must be repeatable so that the results can be measured over and over again and thereby validated. Knowledge produced in this way will also expect to be updated and developed, hence a great deal of PhD students simply take a small piece of their tutor's research and develop it. This (more often than not) entails using the same methods, the same research environment and the results are often easy to predict. Creativity does of course exist in the system. Lecturers can, for instance, be extremely creative when applying for research grants! Further creativity is present wherever there is substantial funding, such as in biochemistry, engineering and technology departments.

The University discourse and the Master's discourse risk supporting the 'tyranny' of knowledge. Both are reproductive, although there is room for creativity of sorts. Both are laden with the power of the bureaucrat, and in both the students are the means to *jouissance*.

The Hysteric's discourse leads to knowledge according to Lacan, but how can this discourse be understood in terms of creativity and *jouissance*?

The Hysteric's discourse: the discourse of desire

Creativity seen in the Hysteric's discourse is closer akin to traditional theories of creativity. The student's unconscious is at work producing lots of S1 signifiers,

> ... knowledge of the truth, comes closest to the essentials of human nature, for we are all impelled and attracted towards a desire for discovery and knowledge.
> (Cicero 2008 [44 BC]: p. 8)

but these do not emerge until they have 'gelled' into some kind of cohesive knowledge which emerges as an 'aha experience' (S2). The primary processes are somewhat different than those described by Freud – somewhat but not entirely. The unconscious is structured like language. The unconscious then contains a mass of signifier chains all connected to each other. Meaning related to these is not static, but moves along the chains causing displacement and condensation seen in dreams. The unconscious in Lacanian theory is not a hermetically sealed box that only gains expression through various disguised traces, connected to the unconscious ones and representing these. It is alive and dynamic. It repeats and it speaks, but it is not stagnant. The secondary process, then, is the emergence of S2. These are produced in response to the teacher's desire. The teacher has claimed that the students have knowledge (and s/he is right!). The production of S2 causes both *jouissance* and pleasure (due to the production of *savoir* and *connaissance* in this discourse) as the students attempt to find knowledge that will satisfy their teacher. S/he is in the position of truth, object *a* (the missing object), and she will cause the students desire as s/he wishes to be recognised as object *a*. All the while s/he presents her/himself as a divided desiring subject. *Jouissance* and creativity are on the side of the student in this discourse. The lecturer/teacher gains pleasure from being desired.

Summary

What might be learnt from this rather harsh analysis, given that the educational structure facilitates both the Master's and University discourses? I think one lesson is that creativity is not necessarily endemic to the educational system, but unconscious processes of knowledge are, along with *jouissance*. Further, *jouissance* can always be appropriated as it exists on both sides the teacher–student relationship, but there is an economy superimposed on the exchange of *jouissance* where we as teachers easily become chief appropriators.

Pleasure is imaginary and related to the ego's mastery. Students and teachers will experience pleasure while acquiring and setting new knowledge into a meaningful context. Thus *jouissance* and pleasure will interact when *savoir* emerges from the subject and becomes integrated by the ego. The four discourses, then, are steeped in both *jouissance* and pleasure. Desire for object *a* drives the urge for knowledge and the pleasure in obtaining it, as well as creativity.

The structures indicate that there is always transference of knowledge going on between the conscious and the unconscious (between *connaissance* and *savoir*). This might play out between the agent and the Other (the unconscious dimensions of the student) or the other (the conscious dimensions of the student) and the subject (the unconscious dimensions of the agent). Desire is essential to the development of knowledge, according to Lacan. He places desire in the same position as the master signifier (with the help of both schedules). The hysteric wishes to be desired as the one 'who does not know'. S/he is incomplete and the students will wish to make her whole. S/he achieves this because s/he, in truth, is the object. The university lecturer desires object *a* (the student as guarantee of knowledge), which will result in a production of knowledge even if this leads to a realisation of lack and division in the student. The master also desires 'knowledge', but in the shape and form of something the student has to show or produce. The lecturer in the analyst's position wishes to elicit the desire to know what s/he knows. All four positions lead to the production of knowledge (conscious and unconscious). *Savoir-faire*, however, is present mainly in the Master's discourse. Many teachers/lecturers use a mixture of the Master's, University and Hysteric's discourses as described here, all depending on time and resources. The Analyst's discourse is probably the most unusual. We might not be able to use this discourse more than occasionally, but there are some things that we can bring with us into other discourses with an aim to modify them.

What's at stake here is a 'sharpening' in the awareness of *savoir* and *connaissance* – to present knowledge or the quest for knowledge as the desire of the unknown to be known. To paint out the dimension of the unsayable real, to be found to a certain extent in the symbolic or the imaginary. To seduce the students with the possibilities of knowing and what this might lead to, knowing full well that the real is not to be known – at least not to the full. Desire is what must be coaxed from the student. The lecturer is a conjurer of images – of promises of the real and the Thing. However, the Thing is not to be found where the student seeks, and in this way the road to the eternal search for knowledge will be opened.

In this process the student will invent and reinvent his/her own knowledge and ego, shedding layers of the past and confronting old given truths. This, according to Plato, is the drive for beauty and for love. According to this model, no lecturer or teacher should ever present the student with 'complete packages of knowledge or truths'. S/he should always leave some aspect a mystery. There should be a riddle, unexplored depths, possibilities to be the first to discover something hidden. The student's imaginary pictures of what knowledge is should be confronted and deconstructed so that the student has a possibility to start anew.

Poststructuralist pedagogy is mainly the way of the hidden, of the unknown to be found. Poststructuralist pedagogy is, if we choose Plato's terms, the way of desire and love. Love of knowledge, love of the lecturer, love of succeeding to understand the lecturer's wishes. However, student and lecturer should not become too close in this process. A healthy distance should be maintained. A lecturer might well find him/herself pursued as Socrates was in symposium, or the student will feel anxiety as s/he may not understand what kind of an object s/he is in the lecturer's affections. Socrates was known to have relationships with his students, and this is the downside of 'too much desire'.

Chapter 5

Lecturing out there with the Other

Introduction

In the previous chapters I have discussed the gaze as a cover for object *a*. Further, I have described how this gaze acts to drive desire and creativity. In this chapter I will investigate whether the collective gaze of students affects creativity in teachers. I will do so in relation to the lecture. Schleiermacher claimed that pedagogy is an art form. It takes shape within teacher–student interaction, or rather within a space emerging from this interaction. A space which can arguably be called a third space, but as this term has been used frequently by postcolonial theorists, I will call it 'an other' space and use this term interchangeably with 'an Other space' in referring to the unconscious as the location for this interaction.

Pedagogy and the gaze

For Schleiermacher, pedagogy was art 'in action'. It develops in the classroom as we interact (communicate) with students, simultaneously emerging from a theoretical framework which the teacher bears in mind, like a map, a rough sketch for the work at hand. He was inspired by Schiller, who also claimed that pedagogy was an art form. When discussing the effect of the gaze upon the artist, Lacan claims (as described Chapter 2):

> All action represented in a picture appears to us as a battle scene, that is to say, as something theatrical, necessarily created for the gesture.... What we see here, then is that the gaze operates in a certain descent of desire, no doubt.... The subject is not completely aware of it – he operates by remote control. Modifying the formula I have of desire, as unconscious-man's desire is the desire of the Other – I would say that it is a question of a sort of desire on the part of the Other at the end of which is the 'showing' (le donner-à-voir). How could this showing satisfy something, if there is not some appetite of the eye on the part of

the person looking? This appetite of the eye produces the hypnotic value of painting.

(Lacan 1964: pp. 114–115)

The artist, then, is driven by the 'would be' viewer (the Other) to 'perform'. S/he shows something (a painting) to satisfy the desire of the Other. S/he performs for the gaze. Even the actual gestures (brushstrokes) are driven by this desire (see Chapter 2) which results in 'the theatrical battle scene' – the artist who paints in a frenzy, covering his canvases with paint.

Pedagogy and art: what do they have in common?

There would at the outset seem to be little in common between the manic artist and the teacher, but let us take a closer look at different types of lessons. There are those which progress according to a careful schedule of plans made by teachers many days before the lesson actually takes place; then there are lessons that emerge either because the teacher has decided to set his/her plan aside or because of some unforeseen event in the classroom, such as an unusual question or a public event depicted on the morning news. Further, there are lectures that do not need to be planned as the teacher has an intimate knowledge of the subject at hand and is a specialist within the area, either because of research or because the content has been shaped and taught over many years. It is after these lessons (the ones where the lesson plan is either relinquished or unnecessary) that a teacher/lecturer might emerge elated, content that the lesson has gone well but with very little memory of what actually happened.

The students will be elated as well, perhaps even claiming 'it was the best lesson ever', leaving the teacher wondering what precisely the students felt was so remarkable and feeling at a loss as to how it might be reproduced. These are also the moments we might suspect that pedagogy is an art (if this wasn't a previously held conviction). For after a great deal of consideration we often arrive at the realisation that the lesson cannot be reproduced, even with similar content. The hour that passed was completely dependent on the interrelation between that specific group of students and the teacher, in that specific setting, at that specific time, an experience which can be frighteningly elusive and, to an extent, likened to mornings when we arrive at work but can't remember how we got there. Time collapses and it seems as if we have lost an hour of our lives, albeit one in which the students are satisfied.

This feeling of loss might, in turn, result in teachers deciding to favour the 'well planned' and well controlled lesson plan whenever possible. It ensures us that we can account for almost every minute in the classroom should we be asked to do so, or confronted by colleagues, parents or even senior teachers to explain some aspect of the lesson, for any reason at all. The problem is often that we don't have words (or a discourse) to describe the experience and argue for its value, even if it is a part of the 'teaching' experience (for most of us). There are many similar aspects of teaching for which we don't have words, but they are nonetheless extremely important, such as when unexpected events unrelated to the lecture seem to cause a shift in the collective understanding of the subject at hand. It might be an odd question from a student, or a classroom emptying before the bell. The room suddenly falls silent, a bluebottle sleepily makes its way across the classroom window as the sun breaks through the clouds, throwing shards of light over the walls. There is a ruffle underneath the surface of the class as 'something' falls into place. When the bell rings students and teachers emerge from the classroom blinking at the light outside as if recently waking from a trance (Herbert and Bergstedt 2008). The experience is profound, but there is seldom an attempt to put it into words, almost as if talking about it might destroy it. In creativity research this moment is called the 'crystallising experience'.

Bosse Bergstedt describes a similar 'moment' in reading, when something in the text causes a break (it can be a change in style as, for instance, when the narrator suddenly emerges unexpectedly in the text).

> Phoebus shines forth glittering with sudden light, and strikes our astonished eyes with his rays
>
> (Boethius 2002 [523]: p. 4)

This break in the text can lead to the experience of reaching new depths in the text, a sense of understanding something even if this 'understanding' defies an exact definition. The experience often leads us to move further down the path of discovery, giving us new interest to find out what other shifts might emerge and how this may or may not change us in fundamental ways.

I discussed how breaches and gaps might set the subject's creativity in motion in Chapter 2; let us therefore leave these two examples and return to the 'lesson where time collapsed', so as to discover if we might find a means to describe what took place with the help of theory and concepts presented in previous chapters (I have already let on that the gaze will play an important part in this attempt).

Savoir: *caught in the gaze of the students*

I recently visited a friend who has two children, a two-year-old and a four-year-old. The two-year-old didn't speak very much, but she stood on the floor in front of me twirling like a dervish, eyes fixed on mine every time she came out of a pirouette. If I looked away she would start to play with her toys, but as soon as I looked at her again she would twirl and smile. If I, for any reason, gave her older brother more attention than she felt he deserved she would suddenly stand up before me, solicit my gaze, smile and twirl again like a top. 'I will be a pretty twirling doll for you', this action seemed to imply, and the nakedness of her intention was quite unnerving, her interpretation of my 'desire' even more so ('little girls should be pretty performing dolls'). By an odd jump of association I came to think of some of my own lectures. Did I not twirl like a dervish in front of the 100-strong audience? Was I soliciting the gaze of my students, then, in much the same way as this little girl? And if so, was this a conscious process?

There are many different dimensions in the 'lecture' which might give us a clue as to the answer of this question. There is a stage or a setting where the teacher 'performs', which is mainly at the front of the classroom. There is a frame on which to write or project pictures and texts. There is also the narrative of the lecture, which might involve 'pure' theory but can also be shot through by examples taken from real life or imaginary ones. There is lighting, which can be adjusted in a variety of ways either for the students or for special effects by the teachers. There is the room itself. Time is limited and preset (the regular use of the same room and preset time limits are both important prerequisites for therapy, designed to induce the speech of the subject). A desk, chair, folders and whiteboard pens are all part and parcel of classroom props, intended to help create and facilitate a 'learning environment'. Windows, curtains and doors can be open or closed, all depending on what is deemed necessary. In other words, everything necessary for the story teller to emerge is in place, although the same might be said for the ego. Is there any evidence, then, for the presence of the story teller during the 'lesson' described above? Further, what might cause the subject to break through?

Let me address the second question first, as I believe it will allow us to simultaneously discover an answer for the first question. A situation causing the teacher to use free association is what might be a possible trigger for the subject to break through, if we accept the theory of the previous chapters. This may arise when a student asks the teacher questions concerning his/her personal experience, which in turn often causes the teacher to sift through memories, describing one after another, thus causing the teacher to be thrown out on to an associative trajectory. Most of the time teachers will catch themselves in the middle of one of these trajectories, and the class is led firmly back on to the planned track (so as to not waste time). However, similar questions from other students may cause the story teller to emerge again and a whole hour can pass immersed in one of its narratives. During these narratives the lecture may also attempt to solve a variety of problems which have emerged from the questions of the students (the subject speaks when the ego is in doubt). Various props in the classroom will keep the teacher's narrative closely on track (oddly enough), as will the students' questions, implying that the ego may also be involved somewhere in the process. The teacher doesn't necessarily sit still during these lessons, s/he might write on the whiteboard or use overheads and colour pens to tease out an argument. However, the teacher will be deeply immersed in the argument, almost intractable when considering the content. Some aspects of the creative process discussed above have been described by Kris (1952) as 'regression in the service of the ego', where fantasy and creative ideas are acquired by the ego from the unconscious and later modified. Wild (1965) attempted to study the process in art students, with the help of word association and an object-sorting task. He described a high number of shifts between primary processes, secondary processes and back again.

Once such an atmosphere is created there is an intuitive interrelation between the students and the teacher. Students seemingly wish for more interesting stories, although officially they ask for an illustration of theory. The teacher produces what is expected, one interesting illustration/story after another (man's desire is the desire of the Other). This shift in emphasis from free association to expectation could arguably be accounted for by the magnetic quality of the gaze. The teacher/lecturer doesn't only produce stories – s/he often creates a 'show of theory and illustration', involving all props available in the classroom, as well as his/her own capacity to communicate with gestures, facial expressions and motion.

> I would say that it is a question of a sort of desire on the part of the Other at the end of which is the 'showing' (le donner-à-voir). How could this showing satisfy something, if there is not some appetite of the eye on the part of the person looking?
>
> (Lacan 1964: pp. 114–115)

This may account for the trance-like experience of lecturing 'out there with the Other'. A sense of operating in 'an Other space' which can also be related to Lacan's claim that: 'The subject is not completely aware of it – he operates by remote control.' Perhaps we perform to the gaze under these conditions in much the same way as the odd pirouettes produced by the little girl described above.

A comparison between creativity seen during the lecture and creativity seen in dreams

There would seem to be a difference between the narratives created in a classroom and the narratives created in the dream, and we need to account

... a song is so seldom a work, that is to say, a thought sung and understood by the singers.
(Rimbaud 2005 [1871]: p. 375)

for this before being able to claim that the subject's creativity arises during the lesson. Further, it is necessary to understand how *savoir* and *connaissance* interact during these lessons as I at least will assume that it does so at the outset. Let us take a closer look at the lesson so as to discover what role the ego might play in the lesson described above and to understand what interrelation between *savoir* and *connaissance* takes place, even if it is minimal, as implied by the discussion above.

The teacher might carry out 'great' work on the whiteboard during lessons. Finding new ways of looking at old problems – new associations – enable a different perspective or a new setting to the argument. This is not possible when the ego is primarily involved. The ego wishes to master situations and to be correct. It doesn't take chances as it is under the scrutiny of the critical agent (the superego) and must answer to its meticulous gaze, along with which the super ego reminds us of being proper teachers with control and command ('enjoy less' is the command of the law). What might other colleagues say about our ambiguous and possibly questionable methods of work otherwise, and what if a student or parent complains? Further, having too much fun in the classroom (working out problems and allowing narratives to take place is fun) might imply that neither students or teachers are taking their work seriously and it might disturb the neighbouring classroom (heaven forbid!).

Student questions providing a path for savoir: acceptance and prompting

The extent of subject creativity in the classroom is probably directly facilitated by the allowances students make for this lecture. If students are fascinated, listening to the stories emerging from the teacher and following his/her attempt at dealing with problems and questions posed along the way, then the subject will be allowed to speak. If students feel uncomfortable with too many uncertainties and want to have a very controlled teaching environment where they know exactly what will happen and the teacher ensures that the lesson plan will be maintained, then the ego will primarily dominate.

The main difference between creativity observed in dreams and creativity which emerges in the classroom lies in prompts provided by students' questions. The subject is allowed to work undisturbed in dreams, following its own logic – rational or not. In the classroom questions are posed, which sets the subject's creativity in motion and directs the subject's activity much in the same way as in therapy. The artist will need to take breaks away from his/her work during which conversation and other types of experiences will affect and shape the progression of work. In both cases the ego's activities are involved as the ego integrates *savoir* emerging from the subject and sets this into meaningful context. *Savoir* supplies the material that is used in the ego's reflection of what it has learnt. This reflection then affects and perhaps changes the ego's relationship to itself and the world, which in turn allows new *connaissance* to develop.

Hopefully this makes the ego more adaptive to its environment, a development that is not always straightforward, as implied in Hegelian dialectics or in Piaget's development spiral where assimilation constantly leads the individual to a higher plane. *Savoir* emerging from the subject can create set-backs for the ego when trying to deal with information from the subject which breaks with its previously held beliefs and ideas. In fact, this kind of information can cause the ego at first to take a few steps back before progressing on to a higher level in terms of having integrated and adapted to new knowledge. There is an interrelation here, then, between deconstruction (when old ideas are confronted and taken to pieces) and construction (when a new set of ideas are created out of the pieces left from the old ones, if possible, and merged with new knowledge produced by the subject). This regression by the ego will not be observable in the classroom. It is primarily felt by the teacher as a loss of control. Something (which seemed at the time insignificant, barely memorable) happened in the classroom, which has shaken the foundations of certain beliefs or knowledge systems. This in turn might lead the lecturer/teacher to defend him/herself against knowledge which confounds or conflicts with the old one. A period of stagnation sets in when the ego busily attempts to resurrect its precious imaginary air castles (beautiful but no longer adaptive). Eventually however, the lecturer will find a balance between new *savoir* and *connaissance*. This will often happen suddenly and without much effort on the part of the teacher. It is as if something has been working away subliminally (even the ego can work away underneath the surface of consciousness), and once it is ready the old worries and concerns disappear. New knowledge will be taken on, enabling ego creativity to take place. This ego creativity will allow for the new material to be presented and shaped in such a way that other egos can be affected and possibly even changed.

The difference between creativity seen in dreams and creativity elicited in the classroom (as I have argued previously) is the prompting questions put forward by students. These questions shape and direct the way in which the subject's creativity will develop and progress. New questions will allow the teacher to stop up for a while in the creative flow of associative *savoir*. When this happens, ego creativity breaks through for a shorter or longer period of time, in which the teacher takes stock of what has emerged, what it might mean and how it will be important for the understanding of the investigation into the next question.

These pauses might be coupled with the lecturer summing up what has been written on the whiteboard and attempting to set it briefly into context for the student and for him/herself. In this communication a

I am present at this birth of my thought: I watch it and listen to it: I draw a stroke of the bow: the symphony makes it stir in the depths, or comes on to the stage in a leap.

(Rimbaud 2005 [1871]: p. 375)

consensus is often reached. Even if the attempt to set *savoir* into context very briefly is not sufficient or clear, both the students and the teacher will attempt to do so and move on. Any student presenting 'trail' questions (i.e. questions that stop up the flow) will often be quietened by other students eager for the next step in the development. They will be promised an explanation 'later' by others who think they understand, which of course doesn't materialise or, if it does, the explanation will be incomplete. However, this state of affairs does not necessarily lead to stagnation. Quite the opposite – the lack of understanding will represent the first stages of attempting to understand the lecturer's S1s, e.g. be similar to attempting the interpretation of a poem. It takes several attempts before some kind of consensus can be arrived at and this is definitely true if the teacher is involved. Questions may then be raised in the next lesson, which will enable a more informed answer as the teacher is in the process of under-standing his/her own S1s fed back as S2 by the students him/herself. The creation of *connaissance* from *savoir* in this setting is social. While the teacher might do most of the work him/herself, there is also a chance that s/he will be affected by the students' suggestions as the integration of *savoir* is a work in progress.

There is, however, evidence that ego involvement can be rather minimal during lectures where the story teller takes over. Some lecturers report a sense of 'losing themselves' in the classroom. They are 'out there with the Other', becoming an instrument of the students' demands and desires. There is a sense of having opened up 'channels' to another 'dimension' of communication after which signifiers simply flow through on demand. The students ask questions, and so answers emerge, from somewhere, rapidly. This experience drives their motivation and causes them to become dedic-ated lecturers, often preferring the experience of the classroom to 'tutoring' or research. These lecturers may also express their surprise when students, for any reason, start to show an admiration for their personal character-istics as leaders (or an interest in them as private people). They have seem-ingly set their egos aside in the creative process. Nopple (1996) called this a 'cognitive style', where creative people learn to tap the unconscious for new ideas by circumventing the censor of rational thought. Taft (1971) claimed that shifts between primary and secondary processes are possible because of ego permissiveness, where individuals have learnt to 'let go' and thereby facilitate the emergence of creative material.

Risks involved in relinquishing the pre-planned schedule

There are problems, however, with lectures where the subject 'takes over'. There is a risk that very little of the 'classroom work' will be maintained unless the teacher stays to copy the work off the board and writes down what s/he remembers, possibly asking one or two students to assist him/her as there is little time for the ego to integrate the new material emerging during the lesson, which in turn implies that there will be precious little committed to conscious memory. Further, the lecturer is often far too drained (even when elated) to be able to make use of the work developed.

Other risks with this form of lecturing become painfully obvious if there is a change in classroom consensus and the previously facilitating environment changes to a hostile or angry one (which is always a possibility when many egos are involved). The lecturer is then very rapidly reduced to a vulnerable ego, having previously thrown all cares to the wind and allowed him/herself to relinquish control, s/he stands almost naked after a trance-like experience when awakening to the cold dislike of another. It is likely to be a rather rude awakening and it might take time for the lecturer to find his/her bearings. It is, however, unlikely that most of the class will have actuated the shift, but faced with a few individuals who have, the lecturer is likely to interpret the whole situation as changed. Most lecturers rapidly adjust and allow their egos to take firm control of the situation.

It must be added, however, that many teachers have their first experience of subject creativity in anxiety-inducing situations, such as being called in to cover for a colleague (who may have a completely different area of expertise) who has become ill. The immediacy of the situation in combination with a lack of books or classroom props might lead to a small crisis. The ego doubts, and just as the situation seems completely hopeless, our story teller emerges to save the day (if we are lucky). Alternatively, our egos take over as we inform the head teacher that we intend to let the students go home early or that they will be working in the school library. Barron (1963) claimed 'the creative individual is one who has learned to prefer irregularities and apparent disorder and to trust himself to make new order' (p. 157). This in turn indicates that on the way to becoming a creative individual (tapping primary processes), we may have to experience many situations similar to the one described above. Adversity, then, could arguably be seen as positive in terms of eliciting creativity (for some of us at least). There is a great deal of research supporting this supposition.

Piaget claims that adaption (closely related to the 'aha experience') is related to adversity in that the former only occurs in confrontation with the latter, i.e. when the individual faces disequilibrium. Albert (1978) claimed: 'The creative person-to-be comes from a family that is anything but harmonious – one which has built into its relationships, its organization of roles, and its levels of communication a good deal of tension if not disturbance' (p. 203).

> Honey is sweeter to the taste if the mouth has first tried bitter flavours.
> (Boethius 2002 [524]: p. 48)

Goertzel and Goertzel (1962) studied the autobiographies of 400 famous people and found that these people often have a history of frustration, trauma, deprivation and conflict in their childhood. This holds true especially for actors (100 per cent), novelists (89 per cent), composers (86 per cent) and musicians (86 per cent).

May 10 – Oh my classmates are terribly wicked and terribly Lascivious! In the study all these profane fellows know the story of my verses, and whenever I turn my head, I encounter the faces of short-winded D... who whispers to me: And your cithara, your cithara? and your diary? The idiotic L.... continues: And your lyre? And your cithara? Then three or four whisper in chorus: Great Mary ... Dear Mother!

And I am a booby: – Jesus, I don't kick myself!

(Rimbaud 2005 [1870?]: p. 235)

Cognitive theory, neuropsychology and the creative individual

According to research cited above, any teacher prepared to take the risk should be able to tap into the creativity of the unconscious. It does seem, however, that some individuals tap into the subject's creativity more easily than others. Is there perhaps evidence for a creative personality which, in turn, might explain the description above of the somewhat eccentric teacher who seems to 'live off' subject creativity? To answer this question we must turn to cognitive research (psychoanalysis does not promote the idea that personality traits can be generalised).

Cognitive theory: traits, personality and modes of thought

IPAR (the Institute of Personality Assessment and Research) at Berkeley, for instance, has been home to a variety of studies, some longitudinal (covering 44 years). Artists have also been studied outside of IPAR (Jung 1962; Bachtold 1973). A meta-analysis on personality of creativity carried out by Feist (1998) caused him to conclude:

> Empirical research over the past 45 years makes a rather convincing case that creative people behave consistently over time and situation and in ways that distinguish them from others. It is safe to say that in general a 'creative personality' does exist and personality dispositions do regularly and predictably relate to creative achievement.
>
> (p. 304)

There are several traits characterising the creative individual according to cognitive research. Autonomy, independence and nonconformity have been listed by Runco (2007); rebelliousness and unconventionality (Crutchfield 1962; Griffin and McDermott 1998; Sulloway 1996); contrarianism referring to an individual's tendency to do things differently to others

(Runco 1999; Sternberg and Lubart 1996); openness (Dollinger *et al.* 2004; George and Zhou 2001; McCrae 1987; Prahbu *et al.* 2008); tolerance of ambiguity (Golann 1962; Tegano 1990). Risk taking, originality, playfulness, sensitivity and a preference for complexity are also cited in research. These traits are present and interact in a variety of combinations. Added to this, traits such as self-confidence and perseverance are cited as present in individuals living off their creativity who are also self-efficacious, self-promoting, self-controlled and intrinsically motivated, all necessary for a career within the arts (Runco 2007).

Considering the research above, it is quite likely that our 'creative' colleagues will behave differently from the norm (in their defence I will add that quite a substantial body of research points to creative traits being genetically inherited).

I write to you! Work now? – never, never, I am on strike ... Why? I want to be a poet, and I am working to make myself a Seer: you will not understand this ... The sufferings are enormous but one has to be strong.
(Rimbaud 2005 [1871]: p. 371)

It is possible that these lecturers may attempt to avoid staff meetings ('a waste of time, very little will be achieved') along with administrative drudgery ('a waste of time and besides its quite exciting to see if the world will fall apart without it'). These eccentricities may be accepted in part because the lecturer is unusually elusive (introversion being one of the traits discussed in research with varying results), which in turn gives the impression that s/he might disappear if forced to conform. Further, these lecturers are often willing to 'jump in' as soon as other colleagues are ill (they are often classroom junkies), yet another motive for making allowances. The same problems that emerge with the creative teacher will most probably also emerge with the creative student.

Research, for instance, shows that the ideal student, as perceived by teachers, is nothing like the creative personality/student (Torrance 1995) even where teachers claim to have great respect for creativity (Westby and Dawson 1995). 'Punctual' and 'polite' are traits considered to be ideal (Torrance 1963), as opposed to 'rebellious', 'contrary' and 'nonconforming'.

Rebelliousness and contrarianism are not encouraged in most organisations. Schools are dependent on a willingness to follow rules and conform to the institutional norms of the educational system. Risk taking (adventurousness) and originality may be met with a little more understanding, as may curiousness, sensitivity and cleverness (Runco *et al.* 1993). The latter can, however, lead to boredom with administration and meetings, which are invariably part and parcel of any organisation's structure. The creative individual's tendency toward autonomy and non-conformity may even cause colleagues and students to wonder if the creative individual is capable of becoming a team player when the situation demands. Confidence and perseverance should be considered very positive indeed within the educational setting, as should the creative individual's tendency to be self-efficacious, self-promoting, self-controlled and intrinsically motivated. These traits could, on the other hand, be interpreted by exasperated colleagues and students as proof of stubbornness and ego-centricity. People who work within educational institutions who do not see themselves as having to follow the law are often considered to be 'messy' and time consuming (somebody else has to carry out the boring jobs or go to the meetings they attempt to avoid). All this being said, there are some studies which point to an acceptance of certain aspects of creativity in schools, such as divergent thinking (Thomas and Berk 1981).

The research cited here is quite worrying however. Creative individuals may thrive in the face of adversity, and so a negative approach from the surrounding environment might serve to strengthen their creative work rather than weaken it. On the other hand, research also shows that our creative colleagues suffer from a great deal more anxiety (Carlsson 2002) and stress (Scott 1985) than the norm, and their work results in tension, even if they originate from healthy creative processes (Rothenburg 1990).

Further, many people who live off their creativity have shorter life expectancies than the norm. Writers, for instance, had an average life expectancy of 61.7 years in Kaun's (1991) study, while musicians had 68.9 years. Added to this, they often have fairly traumatic backgrounds (as noted above). Not surprising then that creative artists are invariably more interesting than the characters they produce or portray, filling pages of glossy magazines and providing material for a never-ending amount of news coverage, undoubtedly providing a stimulating source of conversation in staff cafeterias of schools.

Cognitive research on creativity provides a great deal more than personality trait analysis. Cognitive researchers have traditionally attempted to understand the cognitive processes underlying creativity, and in so doing they have produced models of creativity that are fairly close to the psychoanalytic ones described above, the difference being that they have focused more on secondary processes. Let us first consider secondary processes before moving on to primary ones.

Cognitive models differentiate between convergent and divergent thinking, claiming that divergent thinking is a characteristic of creativity. Threshold theorists consider a certain level of IQ to be necessary for creativity to emerge (IQ being a favourite pass time for many cognitive researchers). Mednick (1962) presented the associative theory of creativity, referring to the generation of ideas and how these link together like chains (a bit like Lacan's signifier chains). Analogical thinking (e.g. a sheet flapping in the wind-sail) is promoted as a source to creativity by other researchers such as Gick and Holyoak (1980), Harrington (1981) and Hotstadter (1985), as is combinatory thinking. Other than this, conscious creative thought has been discussed as a capacity to consider contradictions and opposites (Rothenberg 1990, 1999), or as arising from metacognition (Runco and Chand 1995), know-how (ibid.), flexibility (Guastello *et al.* 1998) and overinclusive thinking (Eysenck 1997, 2003). Cognitive theorists also consider effects of intrinsic and extrinsic motivation on creativity, claiming the former is a foundation for creative endeavour.

Closer to Lacanian models is that of problem solving (Guilford 1965) and problem finding (Torrance 1962; Okuda *et al.* 1991; Runco and Chand 1995). Torrance claimed that 'sensing gaps' or realising that something is missing leads to the creation of hypotheses. Lacan also places

... since they come day and night to rob me of whatever papers are in my pocket, I sewed these verses into the lower part of my under-clothing, which is closest to my skin and during study hour, I pull under my clothes my poetry over my heart, and I press it there a long time as I dream....

(Rimbaud 2005 [1870?]: p. 237)

emphasis on the gap (and the missing object) for creative endeavour. Psychologists traditionally favour phases (developmental and otherwise). This also applies to research within creativity. Wallas (1926), for instance, presents four phases in the creative process; preparation, incubation, illumination and verification. Incubation introduces 'unconscious processing' into the world of cognitive research and is often cited as a part of cognitive models (Rothenberg 1990; Smith and Amner 1997; Smith and Dodds 1999; Runco 2006). Runco, for instance, writes about the benefits of conscious and unconscious processes that: 'By virtue of their being beyond conscious awareness, are able to value and explore those things that allow original thinking. In this light the preconscious and unconscious are not actually irrational; they just have a rationality of their own' (Runco 2006: p. 109). Magical synthesis (Areiti 1976) is considered to be one aspect of this unconscious cognitive functioning, which may arise because conflicting ideas are merged into new constellations (Koestler 1964).

Both incubation and illumination have been subject to a great deal of research within cognitive psychology, which in turn may have influenced current research on intuition (Gruber 1988; Bowers *et al.* 1990), otherwise a rather odd area of interest for cognitive inquiry. Bowers *et al.* (1990) suggested that experimental methods can be used to study intuition! Further, Hasenfus *et al.* (1983) collected empirical evidence for intuition (in terms of primary processes).

Cognitive research is heavily influenced by biological perspectives on creativity, as is some of the research presented in Chapters 1 and 2. So as to discover what current neuropsychological models might add to our understanding of the issues raised in this chapter, I will move on to discuss creativity and the brain.

Neuropsychological theory: prefrontal cortex and the right hemisphere's role in primary processes

The prefrontal cortex is cited as involved in creative activity by a variety of researchers (Carlsson *et al.* 2000; Petsche 1996; Molle *et al.* 1996, 1999). The prefrontal cortex is thought to be important to rational thought and planning, inhibiting irrational ideas and emotions. A disinhibition of the prefrontal cortex therefore is thought to allow for primary processes

Instead of thoughts of concrete things patiently following one another in a beaten track of habitual suggestion, we have the most abrupt cross-cuts and transitions from one idea to another, the most rarefied abstractions and discriminations.... According to the idiosyncrasy of the individual, the scintillations will have one character or another. They will be sallies of wit and humour; they will be flashes of poetry and eloquence; ... they will be musical sounds, or images of plastic beauty ... whatever their differences may be, they will all agree in this – that their genesis is sudden and, as it were, spontaneous.

(James 1880: p. 456)

(Flaherty 2005). Further, the right hemisphere seems to be implicated in primary processes to a greater extent than the left hemisphere (Martindale *et al.* 1986; Goldberg *et al.* 1994), as I will discuss below.

Martindale *et al.* (1986) and Martindale and Hasenfus (1978) found when moving from secondary to primary processes (subjects were asked to write stories) activity increased in the right hemisphere and decreased in the left if the task was carried out over a longer period of time. The right prefrontal cortex is involved in information processing when preexisting patterns are lacking (Goldberg *et al.* 1994) as opposed to the left, which is involved in decision making which is adaptive and sensitive to the recognition of patterns (ego determined, in other words). The right prefrontal cortex, then, would probably be involved when the individual faces the unknown or new situations (the subject speaks when the ego is in doubt).

Martindale (1999) claims that the frontal lobes act as a kind of censor, filtering away irrational thoughts and emotions. Low-level activity would mean that the censor was not working properly, allowing for creative material to arise from primary processes. Findings by Flaherty (2005) confirm this. Flaherty claims disinhibition or low inhibition leads to the individual being flooded with stimuli, which is a characteristic of both psychosis and of highly intelligent creative individuals, the difference being mainly that the latter can sort and organise the incoming stimuli to create meaning. Flaherty claimed that both the temporal lobes and the frontal lobes are involved.

O abracadabratic waves
Take my heart, let it be washed
Hyphallic and soldierish
Their jeering have depraved it!
    (Rimbaud 2005 [1871–1872?]: p. 75)

The prefrontal cortex is also involved in secondary processes. Molle *et al.* (1996) found that a test group thinking divergently had complex neural activity which was similar to when the same group relaxed. The neural activity was traced to the prefrontal cortex. Dietrich concluded that the prefrontal cortex was implicated in working memory in so far as it could extract information relevant to the task at hand from long-term storage areas, even if the information was only represented briefly to consciousness. It provides the individual with creative material, if we accept that memory is one of the foundations for creativity. The importance of memory for creativity is supported by Damasio (2001). He adds that 'having a large memory' facilitates creativity. This leads to diversity, which enables new combinations and rearrangement of old information. Other proof for the involvement of the prefrontal cortex in secondary processes comes from lesion studies. Zangwill (1966) suggested that divergent thinking is disturbed after frontal lobe injury, which in turn would explain why frontal lobe lesion patients do 'odd' things in spite of their IQ being intact. Divergent thinking is not measured in IQ tests.

While Sperry's field of research was not creativity, some of his findings might add to our understanding of the research discussed above. Sperry found, for instance, that the right hemisphere has almost no understanding of grammatical rules and structure (Kolb and Wishaw 1996), which would seem to support the perceived 'irrational', 'unstructured' aspects of material emerging from primary processes. An important finding from lesion research is that the understanding of metaphor is impaired when the right hemisphere is injured. Further frontal lobe lesions may damage associative learning (Petrides and Milner 1982), which in turn supports the 'associative chain hypothesis' put forward by Mednick (1962). The importance of metaphor in creativity has been cited in a variety of different research (Miller 1996). I will discuss the function of metaphor in creativity in the next chapter.

Summary

Given the right circumstances, an accepting audience and questions acting as prompts, *savoir* can and does emerge during lectures. Many teachers might feel uncomfortable with the lack of control implied by the lecture form described above. However, 'letting go' is the only way forward for any teacher wishing to allow the emergence of *savoir*. The student gaze also facilitates *savoir* as the gaze covers the desire of the Other (object *a*). While everybody can access subject creativity, some teachers seem to do so more readily than others. Cognitive research implies that there are creative traits characterising individuals who are more creative than others. These traits involve rebelliousness, contrarianism, tolerance of ambiguity, anti-conformism (none of which are particularly popular in schools and universities). The importance of an accepting environment to the development of creativity in educational institutions will be discussed in Chapter 8. Cognitive theories borrow heavily from neuropsychological and biological research. Here the frontal lobes are considered to be an important area of research.

Finally, research presented here indicates that pedagogy is indeed an art form, for those willing to throw themselves out into the field of the Other ('another space'). It is a world hitherto unchartered, yet pregnant in its presence for every pedagogue and student who has ever been touched by the 'crystallising' experience, where depths of transformation can emerge without warning. These are the moments which sustain many catalysts of knowledge, persevering down through the decades. These are the moments which remind us that there is a magic in our art, lying beyond in the field of the Other.

Chapter 6

Repetition and metaphor

Introduction

In previous chapters I have discussed subject creativity both in terms of teachers' and students' activities in the classroom. There are, however, occasions when subject creativity seems to resist in spite of our various attempts to use mysteries, exercises and other similar techniques. Often this resistance goes hand in hand with ego resistance and the whole creative process stalls. What emerges in its place is the insistence of old well-cherished pieces of 'truth' which the student or teacher for various reasons cannot relinquish. In fact, sometimes this insistence becomes repetitive in a way the student or teacher is not aware of.

> The tumult increased, the invocation of Mrs Moore continued, and people who did not know what the syllables meant repeated them like a charm. They became Indianized into Esmiss Esmoor, they were taken up in the street outside. In vain the Magistrate threatened and expelled. Until the magic exhausted itself, he was powerless. ... Esmiss Esmoor, a Hindu goddess.
> 'Esmiss Esmoor
>   Esmiss Esmoor
>   Esmiss Esmoor
>   Esmiss Esmoor....'
> (Forster 1976 [1924]: p. 219)

When discussing repetition, Lacan described a colleague who stood up at every meeting and exclaimed exactly the same thing (as if it was for the first time). Most of us have had to sit through similar 'speeches'. Students recognise when a teacher becomes stuck in an old argument which s/he fondly airs whenever the opportunity arises. Meaningful looks are exchanged ('here we go again....'). The teacher on the other hand seems blissfully unaware of the reiteration. Repetition comes in many shapes and guises, such as repetitive dreams, neurotic symptoms, rituals and repetitive thought patterns. Even music (jingles for example) can repeat in our minds over and over again. Repetition can be pleasurable (football slogans and chanting during a match). It can also be irritating as, for instance, when mulling over an embarrassing event. Repetition can even be destructive, such as when individuals repeat the same patterns in relationships, choosing violent partners again and again (brilliant students can repeatedly sabotage their results by failing to hand in assignments on time; similarly brilliant teachers can produce the same destructive classroom dramas every year). Repeating old given truths would seem to indicate that the subject cannot forget or release this information. Forgetting is as essential to learning as remembering! Luria (1968), for instance, described the case of a man who could not forget. S earned his living performing memory feats on the stage. He stored memories as pictures, and while accurate, he claimed that pictures would 'jam' his mind. He was troubled by his recurring memories and spent a great deal of time attempting to create strategies helping him to forget. We must be able to forget certain information so as to allow for the integration of new information – memory is not limitless. Trauma survivors with PTSD also suffer from the inability to forget.

In this chapter I intend to investigate why creativity stalls, what causes repetition (the ego, the subject or both) and if there are any means to inoculating ourselves and our students against this rigidity. I hope during the course of this investigation that new information about the mechanisms of subject creativity will emerge, albeit through an inverted analysis. Research in the previous chapter indicated that metaphor is involved in creativity. Is there any evidence pointing to the lack of metaphor being involved in memory repetition or rigidity of discourse? Further, in what way does metaphor facilitate creativity and can a lack of signifiers affect the creative process negatively, as suggested by Antonio Damasio?

Conscious and unconscious repetition: mastery and the death drive

When Freud set out to discover the cause of repetition of traumatic dreams in *Beyond the Pleasure Principle* he described an observation he had made of a child trying to work through the trauma of being left on his own by his mother. The repetitive game of throwing a cotton reel away from the cot, saying 'fort' (gone) and pulling it back in again saying 'da' (there) was, according to Freud, an attempt to gain mastery of the situation, by repeating the mother's absences and presences through the game with the cotton reel (the child thinks with the support of his object according to Lacan). This, he went on to claim, is evident in a lot of children's play. By turning a passively experienced traumatic situation into an actively experienced one, the child is trying to master it (Freud 1920: pp. 14–16).

Conscious repetition: integration, memory and learning

A similar process of mastery can be seen in adults attempting to overcome traumatic experiences such as marital break-ups or the death of a loved one after a long period of illness (however, they have access to language). The traumatic event is repeated over time in conversations and in daydreams, with an attempt to come to grips with a change in circumstance. In fact, repetition seems to arise in most situations where individuals attempt to learn something new. How might we understand this in terms of Freud's theory of memory?

According to Freud, active memories are a part of a large network of energised neurons belonging to the ego. The integration of new information is carried out by 'associating' memory traces with the ego's memory network. Repetition enables a new memory to be integrated into the pre-existing network. New events are compared to memories of old events; if there are any similar memories in store the new event will be easily integrated. However, if there are no corresponding memory traces integration will take longer, causing the ego to repeat over and over again until it has successfully assimilated the new information.

There does, however, seem to be periods in 'mourning' when the memory of a painful event takes on a life of its own, repeating when the victim of trauma least expects it, causing him/her to see the missed loved person in places previously frequented. The experience can be involuntary and painful.

Freud claims that the traumatic experience leaves highly energised memory traces, which in turn explains why they repeat so easily. Well-used non-traumatic memory also represents a network of highly energised memory traces. As noted earlier, a suitable analogy for this would be the grooves left behind on a sand dune after carefully pouring out the contents of a cup of water – if water is carefully poured again over the same area the deepest grooves will become even more defined. The ego (as I claimed in Chapter 1) is a system of such well-defined memory traces, according to Freud. Memories that are used frequently will be more highly energised than others. These will become activated on a variety of occasions that are similar to the events that went into making the memory trace deeper. In the case of the teacher ventilating deeply cherished pieces of 'truth', it is probably very easy for student questions or internal thought processes to trigger the related memory pattern without the teacher being particularly conscious of the reiteration. The same can be said for students. This situation is of course not in the least harmful. It is, on the other hand, inflexible and not particularly creative. There is, however, a problem with this model. The linking up of traumatic memories to the ego's memory traces is thought to weaken the traumatic memory. Why would energy levels in the non-traumatic memory not be similarly weakened?

One explanation might be that the memories are maintained because they serve the ideal ego. In other words, supporting the ego's ideal of mastery. A display of knowledge is a display of mastery, which in turn serves the ego's picture of itself as masterful and in control (a part of the ideal ego). If the truths voiced are important for the teachers or students personal ideal, it may act to block the development of other alternative explanations or models of truth, which in turn may have adverse affects over time.

What then of repetition of destructive patterns, such as students sabotaging their own possibility of getting a first, or teachers sabotaging their working relations with students over and over again?

Unconscious repetition: the death drive and masochism

When looking for evidence of repetition compulsion which did not follow the pleasure principle, Freud found it in the behaviour of those of his patients who seemed to repeat traumatic events and relationships in their life with 'frightening regularity'. He gives the example of the benefactor who was always treated ungratefully by his protégés, and the woman who always passed through the same stages in every love affair before reaching the same conclusion. He commented:

> Why do you whip yourselves to a frenzy, and ever seek your fate by self-destruction? If you look for death, she stands nearby of her own accord; she does not restrain her swift horses.
> (Boethius 2002 [524]: p. 79)

> The manifestations of a compulsion to repeat (which we have described as occurring in the early activities of infantile mental life as well as among the events of psychoanalytic treatment) exhibit to a high degree an instinctual character and when they act in opposition to the pleasure principle give the appearance of some demonic force at work.
>
> (Freud 1920: p. 36)

Here Freud introduced the concept of the death instinct. The death instinct aimed to bring the subject back to a state of inertia or death and was characterised by repetition compulsion. It existed simultaneously with 'life instincts' or self-preservative instincts (ibid.: pp. 53–55).

The destructive patterns discussed above would seem to be caused by the death instinct. Let us take a closer look at the death instinct in relation to masochism as it will enable a greater understanding of the repetition of destructive behaviour in the classroom.

When discussing masochism and the death instinct, Freud claims that it is intertwined with Eros (life instincts) and diverted towards the external world away from the subject (this is sadism proper), while a small portion remains within the subject (masochism). Primal sadism is therefore more or less the same as masochism. Masochism is a need for punishment founded on unconscious guilt that is related to repressed unacceptable wishes, according to Freud. There are different types of masochism, but we will focus on moral masochism as it has 'loosened its connections from sexuality' according to Freud (in other forms of masochism it is, for instance, essential that punishment should come from a loved other, but in moral masochism it is the suffering in and of itself which is important). In moral masochism punishment comes from 'the powers of destiny' instead of parents (i.e. the child's original fantasy). Freud claims:

> In order to provoke punishment from this last representation of the parents, the masochist must do what is inexpedient, must act against his own interests, must ruin the prospects which open out to him in the real world and must, perhaps destroy his own existence.
>
> (Freud 1984 [1924]: p. 425)

Freud goes on to claim that in cultures where aggression is suppressed – holding back the projection of the death instinct – masochism will intensify. Further, the more frequently suppressed, the more severe a person's conscience becomes, causing him/her to be even more careful so as to avoid projecting aggression on to others. Most children harbour angry thoughts towards parents at some time in their life, which in turn results in a fear of punishment (eventually repressed) and possibly even the development of masochism in some shape or guise. It is therefore not surprising when students, at times, sabotage their possibility for good grades or colleagues sabotage good relations with their students. However, this can become a repetitive and destructive pattern. Freud's theory indicates that projecting the death instinct is one way of relieving moral masochism. Socially acceptable techniques of doing so would seem to be primarily related to sports (either participating or observing).

It would seem that pain satisfies the need for punishment in masochism (punishment sought by the severe superego according to Lacan). Masochism is ever present in societies which curtail aggression as the death instinct is turned inward, towards the ego.

> We modern men are the heirs of the conscience-vivisection and self-torture of millennia: this is what we have practiced longest, it is our distinctive art and in any case our subtlety in which we have acquired a refined taste.
>
> (Nietzsche 2000 [1887]: p. 531)

Civilised societies (according to Freud) suffer the consequences of thwarting the projection of the death instinct during peacetime. When turned inwards the death instinct will fuel the superego's critical agency, causing the individual to feel less and less tolerant toward his/her own inadequacies and those of others. Civilisation brings the tyranny of the superego: 'We can always become better than we are, and better....' This irrational demand will drive human behaviour both consciously and unconsciously. The superego comes into being during early childhood and is therefore no more rational than the id. In other words, when the superego demands perfection it is an impossible ideal which it projects on to the ego (not surprising then, the willingness of more and more people to undergo painful plastic surgery knowing full well the risks involved, or the many hours spent in physical training by students who are seemingly as compulsive in their attempts to remain fit as they are in their attempts to obtain high grades). The superego's demands are almost always far too great. These demands can lead to melancholia or even (in its worst form) suicide, when the superego wishes to rid itself of the ego. Not knowing what death is (as most of us have never experienced dying), this decision is often regretted at the last moment when faced with the finality of the act (many suicide attempts are immediately followed by telephone calls to the emergency services).

Freud had discussed a kind of unconscious mastery related to repetition and the symptom in a paper on repression in 1915. 'Mastery' here is related to the process of binding. Binding is achieved by linking up an idea connected to external excitation (current trauma for instance) or internal excitation (an unacceptable wish or desire) with other pre-existing ideas related to traces of memories and material which are unconscious. These unconscious ideas are connected to unacceptable events or wishes representing instinctual satisfaction. They act as a sort of magnetic conglomerate, attracting other 'similar ideas' (representing new traumatic events for instance) and allowing the ego to bind them without actually having to do anything, and then quickly relegate them to the unconscious. Freud gives an example of such a process where a child who is at first frightened of the dark eventually develops a phobia. The original wish for 'instinctual satisfaction' (possibly wanting to own its mother or father) is already unconscious (primary repression). However, the child is 'guilty' and feels frightened of the dark. Being alone is 'probably' punishment – why otherwise is mother not around? Longing results in anxiety, which is experienced as 'unpleasant', anxiety develops originally because libido is 'freed' when the memory traces pertaining to the inner instinctual conflict are repressed. Freud sees the affect caused by an instinctual wish or a trauma as separable from the ideational content. It has its own evolution and development. Most importantly, this affect should be reduced to a signal, acting as a warning against dangers similar to those in which the affect originally developed – in this case a signal warning the child against being alone in the dark. A longing in the dark then becomes a fear of the dark when the child forgets the original cause of tension escalation. Phobic symptoms come about as the result of binding anxiety to an external danger (the dark in this case), which comes to represent the internal instinctual danger (as a symbol), and anxiety is eventually reduced to a signal (Freud 1916–1917: p. 410).

Most teachers will meet students who suffer with neurotic symptoms at some time in their career. In fact, most teachers will meet colleagues suffering from neurotic symptoms, or indeed experience a period of neurosis or depression themselves. Neurotic symptoms are often perceived as embarrassing for those who suffer with them. The fear that others might notice or understand that something is untoward may cause the colleague or student to attempt to cover up their problem with behaviour which is more often than not very inflexible. Teachers who develop a sudden fear of talking in front of groups may go to great lengths in attempting to devise a whole range of exercises, which will enable him/her to make moral claims for the 'lecture-free' lesson. But when faced with a situation where a lecture *must* be produced, the teacher will 'freeze-up'. Similar fears can be seen in students who become ill before an oral presentation of a project, or who shake uncontrollably when forced to make a public performance. This public event symbolises a situation where the student or colleague risks losing the admiration or love of important others, which in turn is related to an internal fear of punishment associated to a childhood event, according to Freud. This is a situation which can be alleviated through therapy or simply understanding what the causes are and working to overcome the fear (research on brain plasticity carried out by cognitive-behavioural theorists suggest that fear networks can be rerouted in the brain if the individual forces her/himself to behave differently, or if s/he learns to understand the mechanisms behind the experience of anxiety). This in turn implies that teaching students or oneself about the causes of neurotic symptoms will enable a rewiring of the brain in relation to the events which cause anxiety, and therefore allow development of alternative behaviour (a creative endeavour).

Metaphor, cognition and memory

It might be argued that the neurotic symptom is a kind of metaphor for that which is forgotten or 'repressed'. Simultaneously it represents a sort of 'remembering' as if the unconscious wishes to express itself through the symbol of the symptom. Condensation

> Forgetting is no mere *vis inertiae* as the superficial imagine; it is rather an active and in the strictest sense positive faculty of repression.... The man in whom this apparatus of repression is damaged and ceases to function properly may be compared (and more than merely compared) with a dyspeptic – he cannot 'have done' with anything.
> (Nietzsche 2000 [1887]: pp. 493–494)

and displacement are mechanisms that lead to distortion of noxious memories. Condensation enabled by associative connections between facilitated neurones indicates that the memory of trauma has been integrated or connected to other memory constellations. Condensation is one of the characteristics of metaphor, i.e. in the sense that a symbol can have several different meanings, metaphor then is also a part of the *process* of forgetting.

Interestingly, condensation and displacement are central to creative endeavour (both subject and ego creativity). Taking this into consideration it might even be possible to argue that the symptom is the result of a creative process through which a subject relieves itself of anxiety by throwing a net of signifier chains over the traumatic memory and distorting it with the help of metaphoric mediation (condensation). For without such a net, without such distortion 'man cannot have done with anything'.

The symptom, then, becomes a compromise formation, uncomfortable at times, extremely annoying at others, but by no means as anxiety inducing as the actual memory it represents. Repetition of anxiety-inducing traumatic memories in PTSD is, for instance, considered by many cognitive researchers to be caused precisely by a lack of verbal processing of the memory of trauma (Hagh-Shenas et al. 1999). PTSD can be a great deal more debilitating than a normal phobia or obsession and belongs to diagnostic category of anxiety disorders.

Let us take a closer look at the relationship between metaphor, creative thought and memory. However, before doing so we must consider the importance of the signifier network mentioned above in relation to the 'symbolisation' of memory and thought (i.e. the coming into language), without which the function of metaphor described above is impossible.

Language, memory and cognition

Oliver Sacks studied individuals acquiring language late in life. He describes a moment of 'awakening' when these individuals suddenly understand the relationship between words and things, after which the whole of their cognitive functioning seems to shift. In the case of Hellen Keller, Anne Sullivan (Keller's teacher) describes

... language opens up orientations and new possibilities for learning and for action, dominating and transforming preverbal experience. We must emphasize that language is not just one function among many. Man does not speak in the same sense that he walks, or eats or makes love. Language is an all-pervasive characteristic of the individual, such that he becomes a verbal organism, whose walking, eating, love-making, and the rest are altered in keeping with his symbolic experience.

(Church 1961: p. 94)

the moment of 'awakening' as that of understanding the relationship between things and words. Hellen Keller acquired language at the age of seven. Her hearing and sight was impaired after an infectious disease which affected her in her second year. She was taught to read and write by Anne Sullivan, a specialist in sign language, and eventually wrote about her experience and took a doctorate, which was rather unusual for women of the Victorian era. Keller (1909) claims in her book that she didn't 'think' in normal terms. Before she 'came into' language, she lived in a world of drives and wishes. Further, she claimed that thinking enabled her to understand and develop her feelings, reflecting over her own emotions and thoughts. Oliver Sacks' research points to the importance of both quantity and quality of signifiers. He claimed that historically deaf and dumb patients have been mistakenly taken for cognitively impaired, which in turn indicates that abstract words are important for cognition, the aforementioned individuals often having some signs to communicate with, but lacking the quantity and quality which would allow them to develop the kind of deductive and inductive reasoning considered 'normal'.

Ingvar (a neurophysiologist) carried out research with a group of women in Portugal, all of whom were unable to read or write (the oldest daughters in families living in certain fishing villages in the south of Portugal were traditionally kept home from school so as to take responsibility for the house). He found that these women were impaired in their capacity to remember words and numbers. Further, they were impaired in their capacity to understand three-dimensional pictures, abstract drawings and long sentences.

Findings of this research are closely akin to psychoanalytic theory, where perception is thought to be structured by signifiers (according to both Freud and Lacan) and memory is largely dependent on language. The importance of the relationship between memory and language can also be seen in survivors of trauma who develop PTSD. They relive their trauma in nightmares and daydreams. The lack of change in the traumatic scenario has caused debate, the indication being that there are memories which do not change or shift in content. The reason for this is thought to be that traumatic memories are stored differently to other memories. Rauch *et al.* (1996) used a PET (positron emission tomography) scan to measure cerebral blood flow (CrB). They presented subjects with written scripts relevant to each individual's traumatic experience and found that CrB decreased in the left inferior temporal cortex, thought to be responsible for the construction of semantic representations of experiences, and increased in the secondary visual cortex. This and similar findings have led cognitive researchers to claim that the memory of trauma isn't sufficiently processed verbally.

One of the main reasons for this lack of verbal processing might have something to do with the nature of trauma (as described in the diagnostic criteria for PTSD), i.e. a confrontation with death, the possibility of dying, seeing others dying and threat of severe physical damage, as well as seeing others being physically damaged or threatened with the same (DSM IV). Freud claimed that man does not understand death since he has never died. Lacanian theory indicates that serious physiological damage will be interpreted as a form of death. If death is difficult to integrate, it will also be difficult to associate to other ideas, and so 'working over' may take longer when compared to traumas that do not involve death. 'Working over' is the revolving door through which the somatic becomes psychical (the traumatic real is caught in the signifier chains of the symbolic), where the representative for an external experience is connected or set up amongst other ideas (and their symbolic representations) in the psychical apparatus. Once associations are set up with other ideas, the ego can use displacement and condensation to deal with the memory (and therefore metaphoric mediation). This would correspond to a deeper level of verbal processing of the trauma according to cognitive theory. It would seem, then, that there is a lack of metaphoric mediation pertaining to the memory of trauma in trauma victims suffering from PTSD.

When discussing memory and 'forgetting', Squire and Kandel claim:

> We are best at generalizing, abstracting and assembling general knowledge, not at retaining a literal record of particular events. We forget the particulars, and by our forgetfulness gain the possibility of abstracting and retaining the main points. Normal memory is not overwhelmed by the individual and separate details that fill each moment of experience. We can forget the details and we can therefore form concepts and gradually absorb knowledge by adding up the lessons from different kinds of experiences.
>
> (1999: p. 76)

Metaphor is an abstract signifier in so far that it does not depict something concrete. 'Prickly like a rose' does not, for instance, refer to a specific rose but to a characteristic. Thus metaphor is important in forgetting. But what of remembering and creative thought?

Metaphor memory and creative thought: a rose is a rose?

Metaphors differ from universals such as 'horse', 'trees', 'cars', etc. While a universal such as 'tree' refers to trees in general, metaphors can be applied across a variety of species and settings, i.e. allow for a higher level of abstraction (important in the process of 'forgetting' as indicated in the quote above).

Luria (neuropsychologist) and Vygotsky (cognitive psychologist) found that abstract words allow for abstract thoughts (which in turn are important for certain kinds of creative endeavour). In their pre-war Uzbekistan experiment, cotton farmers, who had never studied but who were about to be given an opportunity to do so through the kolkhoz system, were given a series of cards with pictures depicting a log, an axe, a saw and a hammer and were asked to select the card which did not belong to the series. They didn't select the log with the motivation that it belonged with the other items (they did not have the signifier tool). In a follow-up study the same group was given information about climate conditions in England (cold and rainy by Uzbek standards) and asked if they thought cotton could be grown in the country (all cotton farmers know that warm and dry weather is necessary for a good cotton yield). The farmers claimed they had never been to England and therefore couldn't answer the question. These individuals were thinking concretely as opposed to abstractly. They had yet to be schooled into the world of abstract signifiers (and the use of syllogisms), typical of most educational institutions.

Concrete thought limits certain kinds of creative cognition, such as those demanded by the question above. Abstract thought allows for a generalisation of knowledge or rather the ability to apply knowledge in many different settings (seen and unseen). Abstract signifiers allow us to understand how the world might operate beyond the scope of our immediate experience. By implication, metaphor (being an abstract term) will facilitate creative cognition.

Deductive thinking is not the only advantage of acquiring abstract signifiers. The word 'tool' in the example above enables the subject to refer to (and visualise) many different tools (hammers, tongs, screwdrivers, etc.) using just one word, which in turn implies a more efficient storage and retrieval system for memory. Imagine if your central library organised books according to their visual features instead of content and subject. Finding a specific book would take a great deal of time. Abstract words allow us to neatly arrange subcategories under the main categories, which in turn facilitates cognition in so far that we can understand how different tools relate to each other and can be applied to different problems (flexible problem solving being an aspect of creativity). Metaphor allows for an alternative organisation of information which, at times, can be even more efficient than a universal (they can, for instance, add an emotional dimension to the storage system). Pictorial metaphors have often been used within visual arts to broaden the scope of communication. *The Ambassadors*, painted by Holbein, invites the observer to reflect on the presence of death even during the most dizzying heights of worldly success and achievement by introducing a gap in the picture which opens up to reveal a skull as the observer passes by.

The lack of movement in traumatic memories (the traumatic memory is concrete in so far that no abstraction is obvious) indicates just how important condensation and displacement is. Neurotic symptoms are many and varied, showing the creative possibilities of metaphoric mediation. Dora, according to Freud (1905), developed a range of symptoms in response to her fundamental problem, her lack of understanding of the difference between men and women. At first she had catarrh, which symbolised the sounds coming from the adjacent room of her parents (during a holiday in the mountains). Later catarrh came to symbolise the venereal disease both parents suffered from. Eventually it symbolised oral intercourse, which she imagined her parent's best friend indulged in with her father. She developed aphonia (incapacity to speak) for a period of time when one of her parent's friends was on a journey (the husband to her father's mistress) and later stomach pains when one of her cousins got married. The symptoms represented identification with men and women (according to Freud and Lacan) in an attempt to understand what it is to be man and what it is to be woman. These different symptoms reflect the creative mechanisms inherent in subject creativity enabled through displacement and condensation. The symptom, then, is inherently creative and changeable, while simultaneously repetitive and limiting.

Let us now inquire as to what Lacanian theory might enable in terms of an understanding of repetition, memory, metaphor and the symptom.

Beyond the pleasure principle: the traumatic dream, desire and the death drive

Lacan attempts to investigate repetition in relation to the death drive when discussing traumatic dreams in *Seminar XI*. Lacan analysed the dream in which the recently deceased son says to his father: 'Father, can't you see I am burning?' (see Chapter 2). Here he attempts to show that behind the mask of the traumatic dream the same mechanisms are present as in all dreams, condensation, displacement and desire. Of the traumatic dream, Lacan states: 'Is not the dream essentially, one might say, an act of homage to the missed reality – the reality that can no longer produce itself except by repeating itself endlessly, in some never attained awakening?' (Lacan 1964: p. 58).

> It is the nature of all bodily pleasure to punish those who enjoy it. Like the bee after its honey is given, it flies away, leaving its lingering sting in the hearts it has struck.
>
> (Boethius 2002 [524]: p. 48)

What then is this missed reality? We have seen in Chapter 3 that it is not the dead son, as the child in the dream represents the dreamer burning with desire: 'Desire manifests itself in the dream by the loss expressed in an image' (ibid.: p. 59). It is this loss, then, that will enable us to take the next step in Lacan's investigation of repetition. I claimed earlier that the loss represented in the dream is that of *jouissance* lost during the Oedipus Complex, represented by object *a*.

Loss is also at the heart of Lacan's analysis of the 'fort'/'da' game presented above. Here Lacan argues the child is attempting to bridge the gap opened up by the mother's disappearance. The cotton reel becomes *the object* with which the child thinks, working its way through the trauma. It comes to represent the lack which also allows the child to master his situation. Object *a*, *jouissance* and lack, then, are all related to repetition in the 'Father, can't you see I am burning?' dream. But how?

Repetition and the death drive

When discussing lack in relation to the traumatic dream, Lacan states:

> The real may be represented by the accident, the noise, the small element of reality, which is evidence that we are not dreaming. But, on the other hand, this reality is not so small, for what wakes us is the other reality hidden behind the lack of that which takes the place of representation – this, says Freud is the *Trieb*.
>
> (ibid.: p. 60)

Lacan uses the word 'drives' when referring to Trieb. Lacan's theory of the drives differs quite substantially from Freud's. Drives belong to the symbolic in Lacanian theory, as opposed to instincts (in Freudian theory), which are biological or real.

> Thus all things seek again their proper courses, and rejoice when they return to them. The only stable order in things is that which connects the beginning to the end and keeps itself on a steady course
>
> (Boethius 2002 [524]: p. 41)

Desire also belongs to the symbolic order. Drives and desire are related to each other in so far that desire (which is one) is made up of many part-drives. Desire aims at the object of satisfaction, i.e. object *a*. Drives, however, do not aim at satisfaction. (In Freudian theory drives can be satisfied by their aim, their goal. There is, however, one exception to the rule – sublimation, where drives are satisfied by something other than the object or aim, such as the creation of art, literature, film, etc.)

Drives move around the object and pleasure is derived from this circular movement, which in turn causes repetition: 'Even if you stuff the mouth – the mouth that opens in the register of the drive – it is not the food that satisfies it, it is as one says, the pleasure of the mouth' (ibid.: p. 168).

Drives are circular (and constant), moving from the erogenous zone (the mouth) around the food (around the object) and back to the mouth again. 'What is fundamental at the level of each drive is the movement outwards and back in which it is structured' (ibid.: p. 177). The object here is object *a*.

> The *objet petit a* is not the origin of the oral drive. It is not introduced as the original food, it is introduced from the fact that no food will ever satisfy the oral drive, except by circumventing the eternally lacking object.
>
> (ibid.: p. 180)

It would seem that the drive is causing repetition in the traumatic dream expressed above, but what kind of drive is involved? The traumatic dream is obviously painful, the child of the dream is burning up with forbidden *jouissance* and *jouissance* involves both pleasure and pain. Drives, on the other hand, would seem to circle around the object to obtain satisfaction or pleasure. Let us take a look at another example of painful repetition where *jouissance* seems to be involved.

When discussing repetition and the neurotic symptom (these are both related to the drive) Lacan, like Freud, points to the fact that many neurotic patients claim to be dissatisfied with their life, but simultaneously seem quite unable or unwilling to give up some of the gains which their symptoms allow them. In fact, there would seem to be a great deal of enjoyment (*jouissance*) and satisfaction involved in spite of suffering also being present. But what then is satisfied?

Jouissance seen in these patients overruns the pleasure principle (the homeostatic mechanism which alleviates tension). Generally pleasure is held at an even level by the pleasure principle. Pleasure turns into *jouissance* once it has transgressed the pleasure principle. It is in this overrunning that the death drive is introduced. Every drive is a death drive, according to Lacan: 'The distinction between the life drive and the death drive is true in as much as it manifests two aspects of the drive' (Lacan 1964: p. 257). Lacan refers to the *jouissance* experienced here as 'ruinous' and related to repetition seen in masochism, which always produces something defective. We are now in a position to answer the question: what is being satisfied? While it is the need for punishment, satisfied through the repetition of painful memories or painful relationships seen in the traumatic dream, punishment is carried out for the benefit of the shady Other, the evil superego which demands suffering in return for misdemeanours as much as it demands uncompromising 'enjoyment' and 'happiness'. Lacan places the superego in the symbolic. One of the superego's most cruel demands (according to Lacan) is founded on the parents' wish that the child should be happy (constant happiness is almost impossible to achieve and so the child will be found lacking).

Lacan claimed that normal nightmares express a fear of becoming an object of desire for the malefic Other (the superego). In the traumatic nightmare, 'Father, can't you see I am burning?', the subject has become the object of desire and is so repeating its punishment and enjoyment. The dream allows not only for the memory of lost painful *jouissance*, but also for the memory of the painful loss of a son (condensation and metaphor).

Metaphor and masochism: creativity and the symptom

Let us take a closer look at the relationship between metaphor and *jouissance*, in both masochistic symptoms and repetition, as metaphor is one of the subjects investigated in this chapter. In discussing repetition of symptoms related to masochism and sadism, Lacan claims:

> When we give these isms we are at the level of zoology. But there is nevertheless something altogether radical, which is the association, in what is at the base, at the very root of fantasy, with this glory of the mark if I can put it like this. I am speaking of the mark on the skin, which, in this fantasy, inspires the erotic practice I am alluding to, which, to give it its name in case anyone is hard of hearing, is flagellation, the enjoying [*le jouir*] adopts the very ambiguity by means of which it is at this level and no other that equivalence between the gesture of making a mark and the body, object of jouissance can be reached (Lacan 2007 [1969–1970]: p. 49).

Lacan, as I have discussed in previous chapters, claims that the 'signifier is the cause of jouissance' (Lacan 1972–1973: p. 24). Here Lacan relates this *jouissance* to marks on the body made through flagellation. In other texts Lacan refers to tattoos and scarification. The latter two do not have to be related to masochism. Piercing, tattoos and scarification are quite common practice amongst students today. The symptom is also a kind of sign, or rather signifier, which combines *jouissance* and repetition according to Lacan. It is in a sense an embodiment of the signifier, causing *jouissance* to be 'written' into the body via the sign (without the visual effects of a tattoo or a scar).

There is (as I argued earlier) a great deal of creativity involved in the symptom (as there is in the many artistic expressions of a tattoo), even if it (the symptom) seems to be fixed. Lacan claimed that the symptom is a kind of metaphor and metaphors are central to Lacanian theory in so far as the paternal metaphor acts to lock discourse into place, supplying the quilting points for the net of signifier chains in the symbolic (Schreiber suffered greatly when his discursive net unravelled). In the case of Little Hans (Freud's famous five-year-old patient who suffered from horse phobia) the paternal metaphor was lacking (according to Lacan), and so the horse of his phobia came to serve as a replacement for the paternal metaphor. By associating everything to his horse phobia, Little Hans knitted his flaying discourse into place. Thus a fixation or an interest around which the subjects'/students'/colleagues' whole world seems to revolve can be precisely such a metaphor that is supporting meaningful discourse necessary for everyday existence. Repetition in this context can be a life-supporting device.

Metaphor seems to be lacking in dreams and daydreams seen in victims of PTSD. Trauma is obviously caught in the signifier chains as the memory repeats, but there is no evidence of condensation or displacement which allows for a change in the content of the dream. The lack of metaphor is related only to trauma, as no other area of the patient's discourse is affected. What causes the repetition of the dream if the memory of trauma repeated in the dream does not follow the same rules as those seen in 'Father, can't you see I am burning?'

Lacan points to repetition experienced in transference when claiming that signifiers repeat. In fact, the whole network of signifiers in the symbolic repeats, but condensation and displacement change the content sufficiently for us not to notice. Repetition, then, is also a function of the automaton, the insistence of the network of chains of signifiers in the symbolic as, for instance, in the example of Lacan's colleague who stood up and said the same thing at every meeting. I have a close friend who gets stuck in discursive chains. At times it is the signifier 'dichotomy' which is constantly repeated in all kinds of sentences – at others it is 'lack' or 'desire'. The repetition of trauma in PTSD is also the result of the automaton (Herbert 2006). Here the dream repeats because trauma has not been integrated sufficiently into the network of signifier chains allowing for the process of condensation and displacement to take place. In fact, repetitive traumatic dreams allow us to observe the automaton at work. As soon as death has been integrated, the dream will change shape and the automaton will no longer be observable or disturbing.

In the wildness and irregularity of the country, a piece of land laid out and planted according to rule looked very well. Later on when I flew in Africa, and became familiar with the appearance of my farm from the air, I was filled with admiration for my coffee-plantation, that lay quite birth green in the grey-green land, and I realised how keenly the human mind yearns for geometrical figures.

(Blixen 1989 [1937]: p. 13)

Pleasure in repetition can otherwise be seen everywhere: in the neat rows of roses planted at regular intervals displayed in gardens and public parks; in the use of certain patterns in textiles; in the repetition of architectural details in buildings; or the pleasure of repeating signifiers in rhymes, music and poetry or speeches ('we will fight them on the beaches', etc.). The latter is probably related to pleasure taken in repetitive rhythms which can lead to trance-like states, as can repetitive combinations of movement in dance. This makes repetition a hard customer to deal with in the classroom, especially if we add that a great deal of investment might have gone into the material which is repeated.

What precisely have we learnt about the subject in this chapter that might allow a greater understanding of the mechanisms of creativity?

Summary

The subject belongs to the symbolic and is made up of the network of signifier chains and belongs to the unconscious. Signifier chains insist, and this is especially obvious when the mechanisms of condensation and displacement stall, causing dreams that are normally creative to suddenly appear 'frozen'. Memory is dependent on creativity enabled by condensation and displacement, in so far that traumatic events can be reshaped and disarmed. Frozen memories that repeat can become so intrusive that the individual becomes inundated and disabled, as is evident in some cases of PTSD. Creativity enabled by condensation and displacement, then, is important for mental health and memory.

Subject creativity is affected by the repetitive motion of the drives in so far that *jouissance* finds its expression in the dream. Painful dreams such as repetitive nightmares are subject to condensation and displacement (i.e. the foundation of creativity). However, they express the fear of becoming an object of the malefic Other's desire and are subject to the death drive (drives are symbolic, as is the malefic Other/superego). A great deal of creativity goes into the creation of horror movies and thrillers involving stomach churning tales of bloody murders. The best-seller lists are full of the same. Further, there seems to be a never-ending stream of people willing to read or watch the age-old story of the malefic Other culling victim after victim. Many horror movies make sure that a small trace of evil survives towards the end of the film so as to enable several episodes of terror. Horror films, detective stories and thrillers are probably one of the most popular (if not the most popular) film and literary genres today.

Luckily this form of creativity is not likely to arise in the classroom as the teacher/lecturer takes the position of the object when attempting to elicit the subject's creativity (hence evil *jouissance* and the death drive is avoided). The Other is obviously an important aspect of subject creativity and will be discussed in further detail in the next chapter.

The ego can often hamper creative endeavour, according to Lacan, because it tends to become stuck on imaginary pictures of the world, clinging on to what it considers true and proven knowledge, reacting with suspicion to information that is not in line with its own well-invested view of the world. This is not surprising as ego knowledge allows us to navigate our reality and survive. New information is repeated over time and often slowly and carefully integrated into the archives of *connaissance*, easily accessible to consciousness memory. There is a great deal of investment involved in acquiring and integrating new information, which is one of the reasons why the ego holds on to its picture of the world. There are, however, other causes for the ego's defensive behaviour. During the mirror stage the child relates to the mirror image first with competition and aggression, and then with jubilation. These two reactions, termed 'primary narcissism' in Lacanian theory, are always present in man's relation to others. Hence the other individual, be s/he student or teacher, will easily elicit the ego's competitive response. This response involves a defensive attitude which is likely to strengthen the ego's attempts to defend its hard-earned knowledge. On the other hand, the 'other' is also a possible source of creativity in so far that s/he is different (when different enough), and the subject thinks when the ego is in doubt, according to Lacan. Thus a multi-cultural classroom should be a good environment for ego creativity. I will discuss creativity or the lack of it in relation to 'others' in the next chapter, including both the defensive and aggressive response of the ego, along with 'attraction' to the other.

Chapter 7

The other/Other, ethics and creativity

On the other side of narcissism and aggressiveness

Introduction

The Other is (as I have described earlier) both another place and another subject. It is obviously involved in creative endeavour as is the other. In previous chapters I have discussed the Other in relation to the mOther, the Other of the gaze and the teacher as Other. In this chapter I will discuss the Other in relation to the radical alterity of other subjects, as well as 'a place' of radical alterity within ourselves. To do so I will introduce some fundamental concepts from Levinas and eventually contrast these with Mead and Socrates. Further, I will discuss the multicultural classroom as a means of being for the Other in his/her radical alterity and as a source of creativity.

Faces recur, faces and faces – they press their beauty to the walls of my bubble – Neville, Susan, Louis, Jinny, Rhoda and a thousand others. How impossible to order them rightly; to detach one separately, or to give the effect of the whole – again like music. What a symphony with its concord then grew up! Each played his own tune, fiddle, flute, trumpet, drum or whatever the instrument might be.
(Woolf 2000 [1931]: p. 145)

Pedagogy largely revolves around interpersonal and intrapersonal relations. While a meeting with the Other can be conducive to creativity, there are certain aspects of the ego's relations to others which can be counterproductive. A meeting between the ego and the other always involves primary narcissism. The ego responds with attraction and aggressivity to the other, which, according to Lacan, is the foundation of all human relations. At its limit, this aggressivity can spill over into aggression. A classroom always presents its occupants with the challenge of balancing creative and destructive forces when they arise. Hopefully most of the fine tuning of this balance is achieved at the start of the term, but at times it can falter. When it falters on the side of creativity, the class might become a bit unruly, but we generally feel the work which emerges compensates for the turbulence. When the class falters towards aggressivity (or outright aggression) we tend to be a lot less sure as to an interpretation of a positive outcome when the storm is over.

Aggressivity is a part of all human relations, as is attraction, according to Lacan, so we can't prevent either of these responses or avoid becoming implicated. Aggression, on the other hand, is a different matter. I will discuss the difference between aggressivity and aggression in Lacanian theory. Further, I will make a brief comparison between both Lacanian and Freudian theory in relation to aggression, so as to discover what these might enable in terms of a greater understanding of aggression in the classroom and how it may or may not affect creativity. Depression, the internalisation of the death instinct as opposed to the externalisation of the death instinct (aggression according to Freud), will be considered for the same purpose.

Learning from the Other: creative listening

When discussing Levinas' views on teaching, Todd claims:

> teaching, is only possible if the self is open to the Other, to the face of the Other.... This view of teaching as 'bringing more than I contain' is of course antithetical to the Socratic method.... The maieutic method erases the significance of the Other and claims that learning is a recovery contained with the I, rather than a disruption of the I provoked by the Other in a moment of sociality.
>
> (Todd 2003: p. 30)

I will argue that she (and Levinas) is wrong (at least in part). While Lacan claims that the Other is 'beyond', maieutics (Socrates' pedagogy) is not necessarily the wrong way of going about getting there, as we shall see. For the Other is indeed 'a disruption of the I provoked by ... a moment of sociality', but it is also a disruption of the I arriving from a place within. The 'other' on the other hand (which, by the way, is the I disrupted in the quote above) is involved in primary narcissism as described in the previous chapter. Let us first take a look at this 'other' before moving on to what it is that disrupts, causing creativity in its wake.

The 'other' is not so much a person as a projection onto another person by the ego, a projection of itself and its ideal. The construction of the other, then, is caught up in the imaginary activities of the ego. Man, on the other hand, is not an island. Projecting the ideal onto an other is a part of the process of 'see-sawing'. 'See-sawing' implies that the subject is capable of taking the other's position and eventually identifying with this other, as I will describe in greater detail when discussing aggression.

We do not see the other, then, as s/he is because we attempt to set this individual into a meaningful context (through projection) so as to understand him/her and therefore control

It is Ego itself which is opposed to an other and, at the same time, reaches out beyond this other, which other is all the same taken to be only itself.

(Hegel 2003 [1807]: p. 98)

the situation or the meeting. In doing so, the ego will project onto the other person its own ideas of what the other is and this is a conglomerate of its own ideal and fragments of previous others. Not that it matters very much as the other is doing the very same thing in return, and if both 'others' can come to a happy consensus they will indeed live together unaware of the incommensurability in these constructions (most of the time). They will instead marvel at how similar these constructs seem to be, which of course allows them to fuel the attraction involved in primary narcissism.

The more similar our ideals are, the more we can feel content with believing that the other is what we believe him/her to be. Therefore, of course, it is much easier to live with relationships to people who have similar family and cultural backgrounds. The charade can continue indefinitely while our egos slowly, without too much unpleasantness, will integrate (through the process of see-sawing) whatever falls outside the cookie-cutter, allowing something new to evolve which in turn also results in the 'other' feeling appreciated as 'other'.

Some individuals are quite willing to adapt to projections made by the other and do not hanker for 'appreciation of originality'. In fact, these others feel comfortable and safe in receiving something to adapt to. However, with time the fit might become too tight, resulting in a strong reaction which can frighten the surrounding others who all thought that a consensus had been achieved. Mr Kramer, the character played by Dustin Hoffman in Kramer vs Kramer, tells his son that Mrs Kramer, played by Meryl Streep who has left the marriage and the child, had attempted to be precisely what he had expected of her for so long that she eventually rebelled. Mrs Kramer explained earlier in the film to her ex-husband that she had 'found herself' during therapy in California and she had previously been unaware of who she actually was.

While we rely on our projections and slowly carry out safe anthropological studies, winning new ground in our own selves and others, meetings with obviously different 'others' that do not allow comfortable projections might throw us out into the world of prejudice (for safety) or confusion (if we are adventurously inclined), or even aggressivity (as primary narcissism implies). These confusing meetings could, of course, happen all the time if our egos allowed us to notice the radical alterity contained within every 'other'. Journeys abroad, for instance, should allow for a great deal of confusion (and creativity), but as many travellers choose to travel with chartered companies, secure sameness is maintained and radical 'otherness' is supplied in small, manageable doses.

The multicultural classroom: Lacan, Mead and Levinas

George Herbert Mead worked with newly arrived immigrants in Chicago. He claimed, meeting 'others' in this way broadens the scope of the social self and is therefore an ideal 'learning environment'. Mead's model of the self and Lacan's model of the ego are similar in so far that the ego is a social con-

I am not one person; I am many people; I do not altogether know who I am – Jinny, Susan, Neville, Rhoda or Louis: or how to distinguish my life from theirs.

(Woolf 2000 [1931]: p. 156)

struct. Mead claims that the child will internalise other individuals' attitudes and norms through play, eventually resulting in a social self through the intermediary of a variety of generalised others. These generalised others help the child to understand the rules of play in different social settings. A multicultural classroom will enable children to integrate norms and attitudes from a variety of cultures, thus internalising a greater repertoire of rules along with the capacity to deal with a greater variety of social settings than would otherwise be possible.

There are several similarities between Lacan's and Mead's theories. Mead claims that the ego is a multitude (Lacan claims that the ego can divide and distribute itself in the various personas of the dream). Mead argues that meaning and self-conscious thought is made possible through the use of symbols, as does Lacan. Man is forced to think when faced with the unknown, implying that the ego is shaken out of its comfortable routine and forced to consider incommensurable reality (which is especially true of the multicultural classroom). Here Lacan and Mead part company, for it is the subject who thinks when faced with the unknown, and not the ego.

When people return from their holidays feeling rejuvenated, they might be full of stories that indicate a great deal of stressful experiences have taken place (it was a strange country and strange people for goodness sake!). However, in spite of all the stress of new experiences, food, stomach bugs, strange road signs, etc., they feel better (who would have thought it!). Many claim that something has changed, there is a shift in perspective, but they can't put their finger on what exactly this change entails and so they often put it down to having been away from work. Possibly this feeling of 'change' is a trace of a subjective shift and while this is an unconscious shift, the benefits are also experienced consciously.

Meeting people in multicultural settings will often throw us out into the realm of radical alterity. Some egos quickly find their ground and rattle up a few imaginary patterns to project onto the other, but many do not and this can, in its worst form, lead to defensive aggressivity, and in its best form into a creative environment for both the other and the subject. Let us first take a closer look at a positive outcome in the meeting with the other/Other.

Regarding teaching, Levinas claims:

> It is to receive ... from the Other beyond the capacity of the I, which means exactly: to have the idea of infinity. But this also means: to be

taught. The relation with the Other, or conversation is ... an ethical relation; but in as much as it is welcomed this conversation is a teaching [enseignement]. Teaching is not reducible to maieutics: it comes from the exterior and brings me more than I contain.

(Levinas 1969: p. 51)

'Receiving from the Other beyond the capacity of the I' refers to Levinas' critique of all attempts at integrating the other into a context of 'old tried truths' with an aim of 'understanding' the other better, as, for instance, when we happily claim of a new acquaintance 'that person is just like X'. In doing so we subject the other person to metaphysical violence. These attempts at making everything understandable and 'similar' are caused by the intolerance of difference (responsible for so many deaths during the Second World War). Levinas' ethical project is precisely to promote tolerance of radical difference.

Receiving from the Other beyond the capacity of the I places the relationship in the realm of the symbolic order in Lacanian theory. For Lacan, the Other is precisely beyond our 'conscious' comprehension. The Other is the source of signifiers coming from the 'outside'. The Other is also a place within ourselves, a place which is beyond the I. When referring to desire, Lacan claims that 'desire is desire of the Other'. Thus desire is 'unconscious', both in ourselves and in others.

A fear of radical alterity in others is a fear of the Other within oneself projected on to others, according to Kristeva. What resists understanding within the other often reflects the undiscovered continent within ourselves, the internal Other. It is frightening to realise that so much remains undiscovered in our relationships with other people and ourselves. Fear of the 'stranger' is simply a symbol for this. Mead claims, when discussing the 'I' and the 'me', that the latter is understandable and controllable, but the behaviour of the former cannot always be predicted. There is something unpredictable within ourselves, then, that will never yield to the ego's attempts at mastery. However, learning from the Other is not only an affair of exteriority, as much of this book has illustrated. Maieutics is also a way of reaching the Other within, in so far that the subject speaks from the place of the Other. This is what Lacanian theory adds to the quote above. While there is a power relation implicit in the maieutic method, it can, when turned on ourselves, lead to *savoir*.

Knowing that the natural stance of the ego is to project meaning on to the external world, how do we avoid subjecting others to metaphysical violence? An immediate answer might be 'love'. Loving others should allow them to be different, should in fact lead to the ego 'extolling' the other's difference from the roof tops. This in turn would enable the ego to use its tendency to be attracted to others as a positive way forward in the relationship with 'radically different others'. Empathy, not just sympathy, often arises in love. Or does it? You probably guessed that love wouldn't stop the ego from attempting to integrate the other or projecting its own ideal on to the other. On the contrary, love invites the imaginary ego to reinstate its ideal in others (according to Lacan).

Listening, learning and creativity: the difference between being-for and being-with

Bauman discusses being-for the other, as opposed to being-with, as a solution. Being-for the other is accepting the other without expecting something in return and without having to understand the other. Regarding being-for, Todd (2003) claims it is a passive stance as opposed to an active one: 'The passivity required to be moved by, be touched, to be affected means that listening lies in a necessarily prior relation to thought itself' (listening without trying to comprehend).

Arne Johan Vetlesen describes the person-to-person encounter as an 'almost passive' thing, according to Bauman (1995):

> Eyes stop wandering and glossing over moving shapes, eyes meet other eyes and stay fixed – and a commitment shoots up, apparently from nowhere, certainly not from previous intention, instruction, norm; the emergence of commitment is as much surprising as its presence is commanding. Encounters are pregnant with commitment and there seems to be no way of controlling this particular pregnancy.

> (ibid.: p. 53)

Being-for demands commitment, then, but the pay-off is high in so far that our subjective emerge when our egos are circumvented and the ground is set for creative endeavour. The more we can learn to circumvent our egos in our relationships with others/Others, the more likely we are to elicit subject creativity in these relationships. In a sense, what happens is the same as when we allow our minds to wander during a lecture. Suddenly thoughts just emerge and make their own way across the skies of our minds, at times meandering aimlessly; at other times seemingly towards a set goal. When this happens during a meeting with another we often feel ashamed, 'having lost our concentration'. However, following these 'meanderings' may also lead us to another kind of meeting. If, for instance, a text from a song suddenly emerges, it isn't unusual that it is directly related to the conversation at hand, although this might not be immediately obvious. Oliver Sacks describes this in *Musicophilia*.

A few months ago I woke up with the lyrics and tune of a song in my head. I had no idea where it came from or when I had heard it (as I had no conscious memory of having listened to it at all). I looked up the lyrics on Google and it turned out to be from an album belonging to a boyfriend of mine from 24 years ago! At the time I was making some much needed changes in my life and woke up feeling pretty good about this. The lyrics started with 'I used to think that the day would never come....'

Circumventing the ego also leads to relaxation in a meeting. Attempting to project meaning onto another person is quite arduous, as is 'meaningful' listening. Many explain that it is not just arduous, but draining. Listening passively, on the other hand, enables being-for the other without pretensions, which in turn allows the other to relax. Cognitive researchers have claimed that creative ideas are likely to emerge when an individual is relaxed. Some recommend meditation; others claim that ideas emerge in the bed, the bath and the car. Bauman claims that being-for the other is a state that cannot always be controlled, at least not at first. Once the individual has made a commitment to the other, being-for is more controllable. Admittedly the relationship between being-for and being-with is a bit like the relationship between *savoir* and *connaissance*. Being-for enables another approach to being-with. Being-with is necessary and a part of human life. Most people would be offended if a meeting only entailed being-for. We do want to be recognised in the imaginary as boss, colleague, student, lecturer, mother, father, etc., and this demands being-with. There are times, however, when we wish to be unique and unassimilable, which demands being-for. The two kinds of meetings interact. Both are necessary for creative endeavour. Meetings with the other do not always run smoothly, as claimed above. At times such meetings can elicit aggressivity and, at its limits, aggression. While aggressivity is a natural aspect of all human relations, according to Lacan (belonging to primary narcissism), aggression is not. Lacan has two models of aggression, one related to the competitive response of the child at the outset of the mirror phase and the other related to mastery and destructiveness at the end (both are imaginary and neither are conducive to subject creativity). They both have consequences for the understanding of aggression seen in some classrooms, as I will now discuss.

Narcissism and the classroom

When man first greets the specular image in the mirror he reacts with aggressivity, i.e. with aggressive competition. But the child also finds the image attractive in its promise of coherency and control (Lacan 1966: p. 307). These feelings of aggressivity and attraction are a part of primary narcissism, the foundation of all human relationships. Aggressivity can, however, at its limits, turn into aggression. Even so, aggressivity and aggression are considered to be quite separate by Lacan.

> For some time I had in the house a stork with a broken wing. He was a decided character: he walked through the rooms and when he came into my bedroom he fought tremendous duels ... with his image in my looking-glass.
> (Blixen 1989 [1937]: p. 54)

The difference between aggression and aggressivity

> People believe that aggressivity is aggression. It has got absolutely
> nothing to do with it. At the limit, virtually, all aggressivity turns into
> aggression. But aggression has got nothing to do with the vital reality,
> it is an existential act linked to an imaginary relationship.
>
> (Lacan 1953–1954: p. 177)

Children who first greet their image in the mirror are relating to an imaginary other. They first feel threatened by the other, as if their existence might be in question, which elicits aggressivity. Pushed to an extreme, it would become aggression related to an imaginary relationship linked to an existential act, survival. During the second moment of the mirror phase the child might become jealous of a sibling who is perceived as having taken the place of the child in its mother's affection. The child will wish to destroy the other (the second form of aggression related to mastery and destruction). Aggression is elicited because the child desires what the other child desires (mother). Aggression is eventually mediated by the signifier (at which point it turns into aggressivity) when the child learns the name of the other child and recognises its own desire in the other. Once the child re-projects its ideal on to the other child as a part of the process of see-sawing which is constantly ongoing, he will recognise positive aspects of his own personality in the other child – his ideal which, in turn, will inhibit destructive tendencies (e.g. that child is called Peter, Peter seems to want what I want, in fact Peter even looks a bit like me, not too bad in other words. I can't kill Peter because it would be a bit like killing myself). Let us take a closer look at this first model of aggression.

Children and adults may at times lash out when they are made to feel diminished or fragile. This can happen during competitions where teams and participants are ill-matched, one constantly out-doing the other, something more-or-less expected in certain sports. We also see this in relation to jealousy, where one individual feels him/herself to be in an inferior position to the other. In extreme cases of relational/sexual jealousy one partner might even

> My poetry has folded its wings, but like Galileo I will say, crushed by outrage and suffering: And yet it moves! – read: the wings move! – I had been negligent enough to drop the preceding page of confidences.... J... picked it up, J... the most ferocious of Jansenists, the most rigorous of the fanatic supporters of the sup ... and took it secretly to his master; but the monster, to make me undergo insults from everyone, had had my poetry shown to all his friends.
>
> (Rimbaud 2005 [1870?]: p. 233)

claim that 'they will go to pieces' at the loss of the other. All these forms are common to the classroom, where competition, integrity-threatening activity and jealousy are more or less endemic (considering the plethora of different relations which can emerge). What causes this sense of fragility?

Lacan claimed that the human child is born too early. Most animals are physically able to fight for their own survival a few hours after birth (by walking or running away from predators). Humans are completely help-less. The child's lack of coordination and control causes it to feel fragile at the outset of the mirror phase when confronted with a gestalt which is seemingly whole. Thus the child will confront the image in the mirror with competitive aggression (Lacan 1955–1956: p. 93). The child also feels incoherent and fragmented by the part-drives which go to make up desire. The image of the body in the mirror will have an 'orthopaedic effect' in so far that it offers the child support, by gathering all the drives into one coherent form – the body. The image therefore captivates and attracts the child, a spectral image acting as the ideal ego, an ideal which will always accompany the ego, causing the child to aspire to its 'completeness', its control, constantly wishing to live up to this ideal.

Aggressivity at this early phase of the mirror stage, then, is caused by man's feelings of incoherence and fragmentation in relation to the 'whole' coherent ideal. While images of the fragmented body recede into the recesses of memory (the archives of the symbolic order) after the Oedipus Complex (becoming unconscious), feelings of fragmentation do not disap-pear altogether (as is obvious from the discussion above). According to Lacan, memories of the fragmented body are stored in the network of chains of signifiers in the symbolic:

> It is a function of the symbols, of the symbolic constitution of his history, that those variations are produced in which the subject is open to taking on the variable, broken, fragmented sometimes even uncon-stituted and regressive images of himself.
>
> (Lacan 1953–1954: pp. 157–158)

Dreams of fragmented bodies can be seen in hysterics, according to Lacan, because of the neurotic's complicated relationship with castration. In subjects with psychotic structures, feelings of fragmentation can turn into symptoms where the subject loses a sense of body, as was the case with Schreber. Feelings of fragility can perhaps also be observed when the subject is so attracted to another fellow being as to be at the point of falling in love. The other seems to be invested with attributes normally belonging to the ideal ego, such as beauty, strength, perhaps intelligence and wisdom, causing the subject to feel in awe of the other, fearing future rejection. Expressions such as 'being made whole' when the other is there or alternatively 'only half' when the other disappears, may also be an indication of underlying fragility, which arises on meeting the master

Timothina roared laughing. This was a mortal blow to me: Timothina held her sides! … Bewildered, burning with love, crazed with grief, I picked up my hat, upset a chair as I fled.

(Rimbaud 2005 [1870?]: pp. 252–253)

in another. The other's mastery did originally pose a problem because man felt incoherent and fragmented when the other was perceived as whole. Man felt fragile in comparison to the other.

The other fellow being, then, becomes involved in our aggressivity or becomes the aim of our aggressivity, because aggressivity is inherent in our relationship with others. When we confront the 'master' in the other, old tensions arise:

> In every relationship with the other, even an erotic one, there is some echo of this relation of exclusion, *'its either him or me'*, because on the imaginary plane, the human is so constituted that the other is always at the point of re-adopting the place of master in relation to him....
>
> (Lacan 1955–1956: p. 93)

This gives a sense of what is at stake in Lacan's claim that narcissism is the 'central imaginary relationship of interhuman relationships' (ibid:. p. 92). Let us now take a closer look at the second model of aggression.

Violence can ensue when individuals compete for the same goal. Parents fighting over the rights to their children can go to extreme lengths. Spouses fighting over property have also been known to resort to violence (*The War of the Roses* portrays such a fight where spouses, played by Michael Douglas and Kathleen Turner, eventually end up killing each other over a house). Otherwise, the second form of aggression is often related to groups locked in competition for the same goal, as is seen in sports-related riots, gang wars, inter-country wars, ethnic cleansing and torture. In this second form, acts of violence tend to be more extreme and calculated than in the first as they involve mastery and destructive behaviour. The second form is, thankfully, not particularly common in the classroom. However, students from feuding factions can bring the threat of violence into the classroom, which in and of itself can be as destructive as actual violence because it results in fear. What are the conditions for the development of the second form of aggression when considering the mirror phase?

To understand this, we must look at the dissolution of the mirror stage, which to Lacan is analogous to the moment when man begins to interrelate with the other fellow being through a process of 'see-sawing'. 'See-sawing' implies that the subject is capable of taking the other's position and eventually identifying with this other (Lacan 1953–1954: pp. 169–171).

Desire, see-sawing and naming: the dissipation of aggression through language

The first motion of the see-saw occurs when the child 'takes on' the mastery of the mirror image. The child originally felt fragmented and incoherent, but in identifying with the mirror image he becomes master. The other fellow-being previously considered whole and in control moves into the locus of the child's fragmented desire. It is not that the other fellow-being takes on the image of the fragmented body, because the other is always represented as whole in the imaginary, according to Lacan, and the form of the fragmented body remains inherent to the child (ibid.: p. 148). What happens is that the child's *desire* is taken over by the other. However, it is alienated in the other and the child cannot recognise it as his own ('the other desires something but I can't work out what it is'). Desire is thus 'projected and alienated in the other before it learns to recognize itself' through language (ibid: p. 170).

> The relation of both self-consciousnesses is in this way so constituted that they prove themselves and each other through a life-and-death struggle.
>
> (Hegel 2003 [1807]: p. 107)

The child, argues Lacan, will then 'confirm' his own desire in competition with the other (I desire what the other desires by adopting the same strategies, i.e. going for the same goals). It is no longer the mirror image that is involved in the relationship. The child has taken the position of master – and in the position of master he wishes to destroy the other who, in his actions, expresses a desire that the subject cannot recognise as his own ('I will destroy the other and so obtain the goal, whatever it is. I have a better chance with him/her out of the way.'). Lacan claims: 'And each time we get close in a given subject to this primitive alienation, the most radical aggression arises – the desire for the disappearance of the other, in so far as he supports the subject's desire' (ibid.: p. 170)

This desire can only be recognised once it is mediated through language, which is introduced by the second swing of the 'see-saw' in relation to this fellow-being. This happens when the child encounters 'something' in the other that allows the subject to re-project the ideal on to the other. Desire becomes revived in the child, but now it is revived verbally ('that's Peter, he is nice, a bit like me, he seems to want my mother's affection, affection is nice, I want it too, though I won't fight him as he might fight me next time around'). Destructive aggression is thus mediated by language through the process of recognition, governed by the law of social exchange inherent in language and represented by the ego ideal, the law of the father.

Once desire is revived verbally, the child can take the other's position again as ideal form – in other words, identifying with the other. There is, then, a continuous motion of 'I am where you were and you are where I was', a motion 'from form to desire and from desire to form', through a series of identifications (ibid.: p. 171). The start of this process during the dissolution of the mirror stage can, according to Lacan, be seen in the phenomena of transitivism:

> The point at which the mirror stage vanishes is analogous to the moment of see-sawing which occurs at a certain point in psychic

development. We can observe it in these phenomena of transitivism in which one finds the infant taking as equivalent his own action and that of the other. He says – François hit me, whereas it was he who hit François.

(ibid.: p. 169)

The other then becomes the aim of aggressive impulses through the process of the 'see-saw', which is the mechanism underlying ego identifications.

Destructive aggression is mediated by language in a second way. Language takes over the destructive function. The word 'kills' the 'thing' (ibid.: p. 173); it supplants the 'thing'. Language enables man to use negation, which is another form of destruction. Lacan refers to the case described by Freud in *Beyond the Pleasure Principle* (1920), when the young child attempts to deal with its mother's absences while playing with a cotton reel which he throws over the side of his cot, uttering the German word 'fort' ('gone') and pulling it back again, uttering 'da' ('here'). The child, argues Lacan, is using negation, in so far as the mother cannot be here when she is gone and vice versa: 'For his action destroys the object that it causes to appear and disappear in the provocation – in the true sense of the word, through the voice – in the anticipating provocation of its absence and its presence' (Lacan 1953–1954: p. 173).

The function of language, then, takes over some of man's destructive tendencies, which can be observed in the pleasure children take in saying 'no' or 'I don't want to' very early in their development. Lacan defined aggression as an extreme form of aggressivity. Negation is an act, a verbal act, which is not normally an expression of aggression when used in everyday life.

The implications of the theory discussed here is that the second form of aggression can be dissipated using the signifier. Writing, reading and talking are all useful methods in a classroom where violence is a possibility. In Lacanian theory it is a question of quantity (enough signifiers for the pleasure principle to dissipate tension), and for this quantity literary studies are usually recommended – they come with the added bonus of quality as well.

For a discussion on the importance of quantity (either dissipating symptoms of PTSD or inoculating individuals against PTSD), see Herbert (2006) and Brewin (2000). Signifier quantity is also considered to be an important factor in the facilitation of creativity (Damasio 1999).

The second model of aggressivity is complicated by a case Lacan presents in *Seminar I*. After stating that man's behaviour towards the other can easily become destructive

A pained impression registered on his face when Kirillov, instead of giving the signal to begin the duel, suddenly began talking.
(Dostoevsky 1992 [1871]: p. 302)

during the earlier periods of the process of 'see-sawing' which underlies identification, Lacan describes the activities of a young child who sets about hitting her playmate over the head with a stone. The child states the name of her friend and states that she is smashing this boy's head. So she is aware of her actions in that she can describe them and she has constructed a relationship with her playmate in 'naming' him. This little girl, who has just recently learnt to walk, knows that there is a 'me' and that there is a 'Francis', who has a head which can be broken so as to get rid of him. For Lacan, this shows that the girl wishes to destroy the other (Lacan 1953–1954: p. 174). This playmate is a fellow-being, around whom the child constructs her first identifications. The plural form of this word indicates that the child has already see-sawed and therefore the second motion of the see-saw – where the desire becomes verbally mediated, or 'revived verbally' in the subject – has been passed. Naming should have placed the relationship on a 'higher plane', where it is governed by language and the law (ibid.). The law here is the ego ideal. When discussing how man recognises his desire, Lacan claims:

> This position is only conceivable in so far as one finds a guide beyond the imaginary on the level of the symbolic plane, of the legal exchange which can only be embodied in the verbal exchange between human beings. This guide governing the subject is the ego-ideal.
>
> (Lacan 1953–1954: p. 141)

The ego ideal embodies the law of the father, which the child accepts or doesn't accept during the Oedipus Complex. Before the Oedipus Complex, language is inherited from the Other, but the regulatory function is not firmly in place until the child has accepted the law during the Oedipus Complex. This would explain why Francis' playmate attempts to smash his head, despite having passed through the 'verbal revival of desire'. In other words, the little girl had not been through the Oedipus Complex. The importance of the Oedipus Complex also indicates that aggression is open to those who have not accepted the law or where the law isn't firmly in place. Schreber, for instance, was attempting to develop his career as a judge, when stress led him to foreclose the law, after which he became ill. Violence in these cases is more often turned towards the self.

The model above provides us with a very different theory of aggression from Freud's. According to Freud, the veneer of civilisation is thin. Man will use, abuse and kill his neighbour if given the opportunity. Accepting the tenet 'Love thy Neighbour' might

I had a little pocket-pistol; I got it when I was quite a child, at that absurd age when one is delighted at the story of a duel or of an attack by robbers.... A month ago I looked at it, and got it ready.

(Dostoevsky 1996 [1868]: p. 384)

spare him, but causes our superego to become more and more severe. Aggression is related to the death drive inherent in man, and it will be turned against the ego if it does not find external expression: 'The effect of instinctual renunciation on the conscience then is that every piece of aggression whose satisfaction the subject gives up is taken over by the super-ego and increases the latter's aggressiveness (against the ego)' (Freud 1930: p. 29).

Man would seem to have two possibilities, either killing his neighbour or slowly 'smothering' himself, as the superego confronts him with ever stricter and increasingly impossible demands. Lacanian and Freudian theory, then, have a very different explanation of aggression in the classroom. Lacanian theory indicates that aggressivity cannot be avoided in the classroom as it is a part of primary narcissism, but aggression can be when using the right kind of methodology. According to Freud, aggression is related to the death instinct and if thwarted will only turn inwards, causing depressive affect – therefore aggression will always exist in an externalised or internalised form in the classroom. Let us take a closer look at this claim and take the opportunity to compare Freud's and Lacan's theories of depression. The latter places depressive affect firmly in the frame of an imaginary relation with the other, just as in primary narcissism it is part and parcel of human relations. The former places depressive affect firmly in the frame of a symbolic relation between the ego and the superego, part of all internal relationships of civilised man (in between wars, feuds and conflicts).

Depression and ambivalence

In Freudian theory, depression or melancholia is caused by ambivalent feelings held towards a loved and lost object, which has become internalised through identification. This can be seen in self-accusations such as worthlessness, helplessness and incapacity to achieve anything of substance, which

> QUEEN: Good Hamlet cast thy nightly colour off
> And let thine eye look like a friend on Denmark.
> Do not for ever with thy vailed lids
> Seek for thy noble father in the dust.
> (Shakespeare 1994b [1603]: p. 32)

according to Freud is aimed unconsciously at the internalised lost object (Freud 1917: pp. 249–251). Freud eventually claimed that the persecutory agent was the subject's superego, which could treat the ego like an object and even attempt to kill it, as in suicide. In Lacanian theory, narcissistic suicidal aggression is one of the causes of suicide (Lacan 1966: p. 187). Here the competitive response originally elicited by the spectral image in the mirror becomes internalised and causes the individual to commit suicide. However, it is not the ideal ego which carries out the self-destructive act in Lacanian theory; it is the 'fragmented' self, which is attempting to defend its existence while simultaneously mesmerised and erotically attracted to the specular image. This battle reflects Hegel's description of the eternal combat between master and slave (Kojève 1969 [1947]). Ambivalence, then, is a part of every relation, because of the erotic aggressive response of narcissism, which is a part of all inter-human relations.

Depression and limited mastery

Lacan's explicatory model of depressive affect is related to the very early relationship between child and mother. The child is completely dependent on his/her mother for his/her sustenance. S/he is helpless in relation to her seeming omnipotence (Lacan 1956–1957: p. 186) and this

QUEEN: Have you forgot me?
HAMLET: No by the Rood, not so:
You are the Queen, your husband's brother's wife,
But would you were not so. You are my mother.
QUEEN: Nay, then I'll set those to you that can speak.
HAMLET: Come, come and sit you down, you shall not budge:
You go not till I set you up a glass,
Where you may see the inmost part of you.
(Shakespeare 1994b [1603]: p. 103)

contrast causes a depressive affect when s/he becomes self-aware during the second moment of the mirror phase, when desire is revived verbally in the subject, as I described earlier. Lacan wrote very little about depression except for its relation to self-awareness and limited bodily mastery in comparison to the mother (ibid.: p. 186). I will, however, attempt to draw some conclusions from his theory so as to gain a better understanding of depressive symptoms. Let us take a closer look at Lacanian theory.

Lacan merged physical and social trends in claiming that the mirror image offers the child a 'semblance' of the whole body where the child previously felt incoherent. However, the child is not actually self-aware until desire is revived verbally. The spectral image forms a basis for social interaction, when the child identifies with other human beings, in which s/he finds similarities with his/her ideal. Man is self-aware, but his sense of self is illusory and belongs to the imaginary. In becoming self-aware, man also realises that his mastery is limited in comparison to his mother's omnipotence. His body is smaller than hers; she cannot be mastered: 'When he finds himself in the presence of this totality in the form of the maternal body, it must be said that she does not obey him' (ibid.: p. 186).

The difference between the mother's omnipotence and the child's mastery sets up a tension, which causes a depressive affect. He is helpless in relation to her. While in Kleinian theory the child becomes depressed because it fears that his aggressive phantasies of emptying the mother's breast have damaged her, the child in Lacanian theory is depressed because he isn't big and strong enough to master as he should like to. Physical mastery, or rather a lack of it, is a central aspect of depression. It is also here that the child will attempt to redress the balance by refusing food.

By eating nothing, a child is eating object *a* according to Lacan, and in having the object he attempts to control his mother's desire (Lacan 1956–1957). Withdrawal from food is a withdrawal from the demand for food. The willingness to respond to the demand for food is closely related to love. In ceasing to demand food, it may be argued that the child also ceases to demand love.

The superego may compound depression in Lacanian theory. Lacan differentiates between the ideal ego, the superego and the ego ideal. The ideal ego, as I have described earlier, is based on the spectral image, which becomes internalised during the mirror phase and is imaginary. The ego ideal is the law, which belongs to the symbolic order. The law is the law of the father, governing all social interaction, and it becomes internalised during the Oedipus Complex. The superego represents a misunderstanding of the law. Lacan claims:

> The Super-ego is at one and the same time the law and its destruction. As such it is speech itself. The commandments of law insofar as nothing more than its root remains. The law is essentially reduced to something, which cannot even be expressed like the 'You must' which is speech deprived of all its meaning. It is in this sense that the superego ends up by being identified with only what is most devastating, most fascinating in the primitive experience of the subject. It ends up being identified with the ferocious figure, with the figure, which we can link to primitive trauma the child has suffered what ever it is.
>
> (Lacan 1953–1954: p. 102)

The superego is an imperative and it can become confused with the malefic Other. It is tied to commands such as 'enjoy less', 'learn more' or even worse, 'be happy'. The last is a particularly difficult command as it is tied up with the child's feelings of inadequacy. Being happy for any extended time can be quite a feat. However, being made to feel that the opposite is a personal failure, or even worse, un-normal, is particularly exasperating for a person with depression. The internalised command 'be happy' causes the issue of happiness to be forever central – something that should be achieved, preferably by everybody, most of the time. Failing this, medication might be the only option.

Striving for recognition and failing: a cause for depression

Depression is caused by man's limited mastery and feelings of helplessness in Lacanian theory. The other is always involved in depression, but not because of ambivalent feelings. Rather it is because of his/her omnipotence in comparison to the subject. There is a case to be argued that depressive affect not only stems from limited mastery in relation to the other, but also from a lack of recognition. The mother inhabits the world of language and will interpret the child's first attempts at expressing his/her needs and demands in speech. Depressive affect, then, might ensue when the child cannot make him/herself understood by her as this is also related to an attempt at controlling his/her and his/her own environment. If she doesn't respond the child will feel helpless.

The scream is one of the child's first means of communication. It is particularly important as the child will attempt to alert its primary caretakers when it is in pain, wet or hungry. Driven to despair by lack of recognition, both children and adults can resort to screaming or crying. Children continue to use voice intensity, or lack of it, as a means of being heard and/or understood even when they have learnt to speak. Being loud or making hardly any sound at all are both means of achieving attention which, in turn, may result in recognition and/or understanding, possibly even control. A final resort can be violence. In other words, a small child might pinch, bite or kick a parent to achieve attention and recognition. There are plenty of examples in and outside of schools where children who cannot 'find words' lash out when frustrated. This, according to Lacanian theory, is not related to aggressivity, but to depressive frustration. While a great deal of violence between adults can be accounted for by aggression, there is probably some related to depressive frustration. Depressive affect and aggression are likely to be a particularly combustible combination, probably explaining some of the explosions of violence seen between jealous partners ('I can't make you understand me', 'You make me feel small', 'You probably prefer others', 'Why should I let you be happy when I am not....').

Translated into a classroom setting, the relationship between mother and child can be transposed on to the relationship between the student and the teacher. Implicit in entering a classroom is the 'giving up' of control in favour of the rights of the group and the leader. Any student entering through the doors of an educational institution will feel him/herself to be part and parcel of this 'giving up', becoming one of many. The individual has some rights, but these do not entail controlling the teacher (although some try). Educational institutions have, over time, realised the importance of giving the individual a semblance of control, putting in mentors, individual study plans, discourses naming the individual as central to all educational activities, but in truth there is a limit to what huge educational establishments can achieve in terms of individualisation (as is the case of any large organisation). The importance of ensuring that students feel recognised for their achievements is, however, well established, as is the importance of students being able to make their voices heard (i.e. making themselves understood). Further, the possibility to partake in decision making both in the classroom and in the school as a whole are also considered to be essential. Enabling individuals to use their voice; facilitating democratic processes; and arranging for ventures where student representatives can bring forward student opinions are all important not only to the running of a school, but also to the mental health of the student body, if we accept Lacan's theory of depressive affect. Using creative activities such as writing seminars, poetry exercises and painting (part and parcel of the running of most educational establishments) can also help to alleviate depressive affect (and not only act to enrich a student's education) in so far as they are mediums of expression where students who might have difficulties making their voice heard under usual circumstances get another chance to communicate and gain recognition. Naturally, students will always have periods when they feel that they are not recognised enough, however hard we try to arrange our activities to ensure this doesn't happen. Noisy behaviour, loud speech, unruliness, sudden weight loss or attempts at complete invisibility can be signs that a student is looking for attention to alleviate depressive affect.

Summary

Meetings with others/Others can lead to subject creativity, but also to the emergence of aggressivity (a part of primary narcissism) and depressive affect. Levinas points to the risks of attempting to integrate others by comparing them to already-known individuals in our surroundings. This, he claims, is doing 'metaphysical violence' to the other. There are always aspects of the other which are beyond and we must accept this, not struggle against it. The other presents us with an opportunity for learning, which is particularly apparent in the multicultural classroom. The problems of integration belong to the ego. The ego in Lacanian theory lives in a world which it has built up through see-sawing, projecting its own ideals and its own internal world onto others. If we are to learn from the other in the way Levinas indicates, the subject must be involved (as opposed to the ego), not only as a weaver of narratives, but also as a listener. This demands a certain way of being (being-for as opposed to being-with) which can be learnt over time (according to Bauman). Problems which emerge during 'meetings' with others are often related to primary narcissism.

Aggressivity is caused originally by feelings of incoherence and fragmentation, or fragility in relation to the coherent master. After the Oedipus Complex the memory of the fragmented body recedes into the recesses of the symbolic and is expressed in images, which are unconscious. However, it is likely that echoes of the memory remain in terms of feelings of fragility or weakness when faced with the ideal in the other. Aggressivity is also related to mastery and destructive behaviour. Both forms of aggressivity can turn into aggression. The former often emerges during competitions when the participants are ill-matched. As classroom activities invariably involve competition in one way or another (even if students are directed to compete with themselves and avoid comparing themselves to others) and brilliant students will almost always be present, it is difficult to avoid aggression completely. Luckily, this form of aggression tends to be relatively mild and easy to manage. The second form of aggression, arising from the last and final phases of the mirror stage is, however, more severe and unusual. It can be dissipated by the signifier, so communicating verbally in any form, writing and reading are likely to alleviate problems in classrooms experiencing aggressive tension.

The implication of Lacan's theory of depressive affect as developed in the preceding paragraphs is that man will have to live with depressive affect in relation to the other, as well as with ambivalent feelings of love and hate, as depressive affect is a consequence of becoming self-aware. Lacanian theory indicates that depression is not conducive to subject creativity as the ego is locked into an imaginary relationship with the other, where s/he is striving for recognition. However, creative activities can act as an antidote for both aggression and depression. In Freudian theory, on the other hand, the door is open to creativity through sublimation where the loved lost and internalised object is extolled in poetry and other texts. Paradoxically, the original external object becomes the aim of creative endeavour. Needless to add, creative endeavour which recognises a creative source existing within all people, thus toning down competition, is a powerful antidote when parts of a classroom heat up (to the point of boiling) or cool down (to the point of freezing). The recognition that aggressivity (caused by competition) and depressive affect (caused by feelings of helplessness) are a 'normal part' of school life (and not signs of failure) where 'individualisation' is an ideal but not completely realisable, might enable teachers to discuss these aspects of their classrooms more readily and openly.

Chapter 8

Methodology

Introduction

'Don't think, just tell me what comes up', Parveen exclaimed and confronted me with a series of pictures in a modern art gallery (I can't quite remember where). Perusing modern art galleries has certainly not been one of my favourite activities in the past. However, after being sent to a whole range of art exhibitions, none of which I found particularly titillating, I learned to appreciate the quality of certain pictures and their capacity to elicit creative thought, whether it be *connaissance* or *savoir*. In this chapter I will discuss how visual arts and literature can be used to develop creative methods. I will present some new methods and summarise and elaborate on some previously presented others. Further, I will discuss the importance of student–teacher relations for the development of a creative organisational climate, along with other factors that facilitate the success of methods presented and discussed here.

Art and methodology

My reaction to a great deal of the exhibitions which I was directed to visit was initially irritation and frustration (as is the case for many first-time readers of Lacan's texts). More often than not I was angry that my time was being wasted. I could not bring myself to find anything to admire or integrate in the pictures. Naturally, in hindsight I understand that Parveen selected exhibitions carefully. But at the time I thought most of the art was a joke being played on the world, supported by critics who had to survive by ratcheting up the reputation of one or other artist. As most modern art lovers can tell, I was quite a philistine.

Modern art

Modern art can be a quick route to integrating a dialogue between *connaissance* and *savoir* for those who are sensitive to pictorial arts, though it can take both time and patience. For me it has been an acquired taste and therefore I have to sit for at least 30 minutes in front of a painting before I stop being frustrated or analytic, using all my prior knowledge of the artist in an attempt to understand what precisely s/he was trying to achieve (though it is possible to circumvent the ego's critical censor by quickly responding without thinking, as in the example above). Once the interpretation phase is over and my mind starts to wander, I do eventually achieve productive and creative thought. This is not a method I personally prefer as I am not particularly pictorially inclined, but I know it works very well for others.

Many modern artists have consciously worked to avoid the interpretive process. Francis Bacon used to destroy paintings if they could be interpreted. Interviews with the artist also indicate that he was aiming at the real when creating his work, using graining techniques and flesh as subject matter. Žižek has written about the attempt by modern art to replace the sublime with the real, old bicycles, dismembered body parts and faeces taking the place of beautiful landscapes and female bodies. In fact, Žižek claims that the space (the gap or the lack) that object *a* depicts is closing up. People get easily exchangeable replacements, thus the function of the Thing is threatened. Modern art attempts to display the 'real' so as to maintain the space.

Modern art easily lends itself to creative activities in any subject, much due to the humour, fun and rebellion which it often conveys, but also because it includes electrical installations, IT and a variety of other technologies (physics, maths and chemistry can therefore be included). Miro's bounce, Klee's regularity and Hokney's cool are often appreciated, especially by younger students. Installations are also sources of inspiration or facilitation. Most importantly, art which is confusing, repetitive or which resists any immediate interpretation is useful.

Ramachandran and Hirstein (1999) claimed that:

> some types of art such as cubism are activating the brain mechanisms in such a way as to tap or even caricature certain innate form primitives which we do not yet fully understand.... Many artists may be unconsciously producing heightened activity in the 'form areas' in a manner that is not obvious to the conscious mind.
>
> (pp. 20–21)

This is quite contrary to theory which points to the pleasure of art being connected to *connaissance*. Martindale (1988) argues that it is the construction of meaning in relation to art that results in pleasure, thus emphasising content as opposed to form. Lacan emphasises the importance of light (as opposed to content or form) when discussing desire and *jouissance* in relation to art, specifically art where light converges onto or is seen to radiate out from one location in the picture. This source of light acts to cover the gaze. Lacan was sitting in a boat with a group of fishers outside Marseille when one of the men pointed towards a tin bobbing up and down on the water reflecting the sun, and exclaimed laughingly 'you see it but it doesn't see you'. The gaze is a cover for object *a*, but it is also the gaze which causes the artist to create, as described in Chapter 3. The light, then, in the picture can have certain effects on the subject.

Writing and reading: media and films

Undoubtedly many modern writers attempt to avoid the interpretive process, just like modern painters. Lacan used a variety of techniques to confuse his readers (see Chapter 3). Double negations have been used by a great many writers over the years, as they tend to confuse the reader and throw them off the path of interpretation. Lacan also uses a method whereby he seems to attempt to answer questions which have arisen at the outset of a seminar without actually producing any definite answers towards the end. However, an answer of sorts is often embedded somewhere in the text and the reader will simply have to reread the book a couple of times to find it, or alternatively read several seminars for the same end. There are also times when he seems to switch subjects or lose interest in the investigation at hand, only to pick it up again a few chapters later. Lacan's texts are almost predictably unpredictable, infused with humour, references to classical literature interwoven with philosophical meanderings, case studies, dialogues with famous people in the seminar audience, riddles, etc.

Bergstedt (1998) argues that the 'methods' discussed above create a rupture in the text at hand which allows a gap to open up, eliciting the subject's creativity. These are experienced as a shift in understanding where certain aspects of the text suddenly fall in to place, leading to the 'aha experience'. In other words, the ruptures allow for an 'opening up' towards the unconscious which is often consciously experienced as a change in awareness. This can result in a deep sense of change in the reader, which cognitive psychologists term 'the crystallising experience'. Some books touch us more in terms of depth and dignity than others, and the reason for this is not always consciously accessible. Watson became determined to uncover the workings of the gene after reading *What Is Life* (a crystallising experience, in other words).

Creative writing, popular with many English literature teachers, can be primed to facilitate subject creativity. Using a nonsensical subject matter such as 'the sound of one hand clapping', and asking students to respond immediately (thus avoiding analytic thought) are some of the techniques used to access *savoir* during writing exercises. However, students can also access primary processes when asked to use free association to create ideas for a story, coupled with instructions to be 'original in their writing'. Martindale *et al.* (1986) studied primary processes with the help of creative writing, measuring left and right hemisphere activity. They found that primary processes were related to high right-hemisphere activities and low left-hemisphere activities (so-called basal asymmetry). These changes were positively related to primary processes when measurements were stable over a long period of time.

Poetry can be written according to free associative techniques, where the text relates closely to the words emerging during free association. In some modern poetry it is difficult to judge if the author has created his/her verses to avoid any form of interpretation, or if the words have been recorded as they arise during free association. Socrates wrote (as mentioned earlier) that poets are like diviners: they don't always know the meaning of their own texts. Poetry, then, may be the result of subject creativity, but can also elicit the same.

A film is a combination of text and image. Therefore any of the techniques for creating gaps and ruptures should be applicable. However, films involve moving images, which immediately implicates the ego. Movement demands unconscious and conscious processing. This is a necessary part of perception and it is therefore very difficult to disentangle the ego from its interpretive process, added to which it is challenged with the task of interpreting sound and text simultaneously (the same can be said of theatre, ballet and many musical concerts). Music, which often is used to evoke, enhance or maintain emotions, also belongs to the domain of the imaginary ego, according to Lacan. Static pictures and texts provide the ego (here conscious processing of stimuli) with somewhat less challenges, and therefore it is easier to circumvent the ego, allowing for the subject to emerge. An additional difficulty with films is that they more often than not convey a story, which in turn is conducive to *connaissance* as opposed to *savoir*. This is not to say that films never elicit *savoir* or that films cannot create a sense of change in the viewer. The crystallising moments achieved by films, however, are more often than not created through recognition. Either the viewer recognises him/herself in one of the characters of the film, or recognises certain situations.

Films are a great deal more expensive to make than a normal painting, and therefore any film maker who wishes to survive will have to think twice before creating a completely inexplicable and confusing story such as would be necessary for subject creativity to emerge (theatre, ballet and musical concerts are, on the other hand, somewhat less expensive and in many countries state-subsidised, allowing for diversification and productions which might be a little more conducive to subject creativity). There are art films, but these seldom survive to reach the big screen and are therefore difficult to access for teachers. Most confusing films that do reach the big screen are often horror movies or thrillers, and are therefore deemed unsuitable for the classroom. Alternative film is often considered unsuitable due to content. I have even had to deal with shocked silence in a classroom full of PhD students and lecturers after viewing a Cronenberg or a Passolini film after the most meticulous planning. The ego inevitably seems to get involved one way or another, and with it strong emotions which tend to block subject creativity (this is also a problem with music). Parveen used films to illustrate theory, and as such they worked very well. I am not aware that she ever used them to elicit creative endeavour.

Free association, creativity exercises, discourse analysis and deconstruction

Free association is often used by teachers as a part of competitions, charades and other similar exercises. Parveen's task, as described above, was also one of free association even if I eventually chose a longer and more laborious route to subject creativity. I mentioned Jack Norin's exercise earlier (Chapter 3) as I have used it in most of my own classes and will therefore briefly describe it below.

Jack Norin's creativity exercise

It is important for any teacher attempting to work with the creativity of the subject to avoid the ego's tendency to censor ideas which are too unusual or socially unacceptable. Runco (1985) discusses the problems of creative inhibition due to social pressure in groups. A great deal of time at the beginning of Norin's exercise is spent on explaining why critique of the self and of others is damaging to creativity. It is in fact a part of the exercise to compete with others in avoiding the critical censor. People are seated in groups of four. They are given a creative task to carry out within a time limit (three minutes), such as suggesting different ways of reusing and recycling old milk cartons. To win the competition they must get the longest list of suggestions (there is a lower limit, often 15 items to start with). One person is selected to write down the group's suggestions. The first task is followed by a second, where the lower level cut off point is determined by the results of the best group. The second is followed by a third on the same principle. After each three-minute period the various groups present their results and the winning group is given a round of applause. After the third round the groups have normally reached their maximum output and they are given a problem to solve (for the whole class) or a project to plan. The best solutions (chosen by each group) are put up on a list and the members of the different groups walk around, discussing each others' solutions. At the end of the exercise all subgroups come together and choose three good suggestions to work with and develop. I have used this exercise on a variety of occasions and with a variety of age groups. It always leads to laughter and a loss of self-awareness as the suggestions become more and more relaxed.

Free association is closely related to brainstorming. The former aims at *savoir* and the latter at *connaissance*. However, *savoir* is also likely to emerge during brainstorming sessions. According to Runco, brainstorming exercises should generally follow three guidelines: 1) avoid judgement, 2) focus on the quantity of ideas and not their quality – produce as many ideas as possible, and 3) try finding ideas via piggy backing or hitchhiking (Runco 2007: pp. 166–167). The last guideline refers to using other people's ideas (by mutual consent). Guidelines described by Runco address *connaissance*. However, they also facilitate *savoir* when merged together, as described in the exercise above.

Another way of accessing primary processes or *savoir* for creative endeavour is to keep a dream diary, writing down whatever can be remembered immediately after waking. The content of the dream diary can later be used in creative writing. Mary Shelley's famous book, *Frankenstein*, was developed in this way, and Blake used dreams as a motive for his own paintings.

Harman and Rheingold (1984) have described several methods that are independent of art, literature and media. They suggest that questions can be aimed directly at the unconscious, which might then act as an 'internal teacher, helper or guide'. Guided imagery can be used to access the unusual imagery that emerges in dreams, affirmation in terms of repeating self-instructions can act to programme the unconscious in a wanted direction (creativity) and alert relaxation facilitates the emergence of primary creativity (Wallas 1926) by relaxing the internal censors (Harman and Rheingold 1984).

There is an interplay between *savoir* and *connaissance* in creative endeavour most of the time, although the process can be mostly primary to start with and eventually move into secondary as the ideas (Noy 1969) which emerge are set into place and structured so as to be integrated and presentable (Dudek and Verreault 1989). Wild (1965) attempted to study the process in art students with the help of word association and an object-sorting task. He described a high number of shifts between primary processes and secondary processes and back again.

Discourse analysis and deconstruction

When creativity and *savoir* fail to emerge in spite of having tried a variety of different methodologies, it may be necessary to carry out discourse analysis and/or deconstruction. Repetition of well-cherished truths or 'knowledge' in which the ego has invested heavily over the years can block creativity, making us self-blind. Discourse analysis can help to highlight areas that are particularly resistant and/or insistent. If we notice that a student's work tends to gravitate towards the same subject over and over again (in a variety of shapes and guises) it is possible to ask the student to carry out an analysis of his/her own work, highlighting all dichotomies that exist within the text or are implied by the text. Derrida argues that language is a limited medium, tending to lock our expression of knowledge and/or opinions (i.e. we are dependent on our vocabulary) within the framework of discourse: dichotomies existing within a discourse effects linguistic expression. By analysing and highlighting dichotomies within our own texts we come to understand the discourse (or discourses, as there can be several) we are moving in and how these affect our thinking and linguistic expression. By 'crossing over' one concept in a dichotomy and exchanging it for something else, it is possible to create new perspectives on a previously 'fixed' narrative. Derrida claims that one of the concepts is almost always given a greater value than the other (often rather gratuitously). This hierarchy should be reversed during deconstruction (however, the previously less-valued concept should not be 'favoured'). Lenz Taguchi (2000) carried out an analysis and deconstruction on narratives present within the discourse of kindergarten teachers (in her doctoral thesis). She crossed out the word 'security', which emerged as dominant, and replaced it with a new perspective in relation to 'insecurity'. Once this was done and the chosen concept was completely exchanged or reinterpreted, new possibilities evolved. Discourse analysis and deconstruction do not in and of themselves elicit *savoir* or subject creativity, but they clear the way for creative endeavour in so far that they enable an insight into our own favoured narratives and suggest ways in which these could be changed.

Climate: creative environments

The methods discussed above are aimed primarily at individuals and can be used anywhere (by anybody). I will now go on to discuss the importance of the relationship and climate (created) between teachers and students, as well as organisational climate.

While certain types of methodology can facilitate creative endeavour, classroom climate can be instrumental in the failure or success of these methodologies. Ekvall and Ryhammar (1999) claim that organisations aiming to facilitate creativity must provide their members with (meaningful) challenges, initiative, a supportive environment for new ideas, freedom and a permissive environment for risk taking and trust. Amabile (Amabile and Gryskiewicz 1989) adds recognition as an important dimension.

A permissive open environment which allows for eccentricities and novel ideas will obviously be more conducive to subject creativity than a rigid, closed environment that demands adherence to rules and conformism. Schools are dependent to some degree on conformism and a capacity to follow rules, but this does not preclude school environments from being permissive and open to unusual ideas. Much depends on the leader of the classroom. Parveen's classroom was creative because she clearly showed that creative, innovative and original ideas would be supported – in fact these were expected. Further, we were expected to take risks intellectually and Parveen trusted students to develop new theories. I remember worrying about the lack of psychoanalytic models of PTSD and being directed to create my own. We learnt to challenge and question our own assumptions or long-held and cherished 'truths' routinely, which in turn threw us into uncharted waters. This could be both confusing and frightening. However, the subject thinks when the ego is in doubt. Confusion was very definitely an ally when aiming at *savoir*, and it was something most of us had to learn to live with for longer periods of time rather than shorter. The greatest struggle was perhaps letting *savoir* emerge without allowing self-criticism to squelch it. It was often a case of relaxing as ideas welled forth. I spent a great deal of time doing my work (i.e. letting ideas emerge) in bed or in the bath. During the final year I lived for six months in Thailand and wrote my final chapters lying on a sunbed under a parasol. Taft (1971) called the capacity to let go, allowing for primary processes to emerge, 'ego permissiveness'.

According to cognitive research, most of the things that were natural to our classroom are essential to a creative climate: openness, flexibility, support of original ideas, trust, allowance for eccentricity, etc. Parnes (1967) has written about the importance of 'making it happen'. Runco (2007) mentions the questioning of assumptions, as well as the emergence of creative ideas while travelling and experiencing relaxed states such as being in bed and the bath. Root-Bernstein (1989) claimed that the creation of paradoxes, considering things that are generally thought to be mad or impossible, are some of the tactics used by discoverers. Playful, permissive climates are also considered to be conducive to creativity (Wallach and Kogan 1965).

Student–teacher relations and creative climate in the four discourses

Cognitive research points to the importance of the relationship between student and teacher, the teacher being a role model for the student, establishing 'what goes' as well as setting the agenda – something Lacan emphasises in the four discourses. The master, for instance, literally squelches subject creativity (more often than not), as onus is placed on productivity, normative behaviour (work), quantitative measurement (grades) and the preservation of rules. Excellence demanded by the teacher is measured and graded, seldom referring to original thought or 'thinking outside the box'. There are masters who demand creative work but would not recognise *savoir* even if it jumped up and bit them, because the teacher/lecturer doesn't actually understand the object of his/her desire (object *a*).

The relationship with the university lecturer fairs only marginally better. The students are the 'guarantors' of knowledge (in fact they are object *a*), the kind of knowledge necessary for the lecturer's own research and the survival of the university. The lecturer is an 'amasser' of knowledge (primarily *connaissance*), driven to know more and more. Work produced by PhD students, then, does not have to be creative and is (due to the methods supported by research at the university) often reproductive, produced to support the lecturer's own research (if s/he has anything to do with it). Where the lecturer is dependent on creative endeavour, be it *savoir* or *connaissance*, subject creativity can and does emerge. This, however, is usually most evident at the 'idea stage' of a thesis.

The lecturer/teacher within the Hysteric's discourse develops a creative climate precisely due to his/her interest in the student–teacher relationship. In openly admitting that s/he is 'lacking' (i.e. does not have 'complete knowledge' or control), this lecturer allows for an environment where students are made to feel that they are as likely as anybody else to have whatever their lecturer is searching for (object *a* is, in this case, knowledge). This environment or climate is empowering and allows for risk taking and a 'just let it happen' approach. The lecturer is seemingly searching for answers which never quite materialise, but students will become very creative in attempting to provide him/her with a solution, and in doing so both *savoir* and *connaissance* will emerge. Where *savoir* is concerned, students will be left to their own devices in interpreting and analysing their production. The lecturer does not provide any answers, knowledge is a process, there is no final destination and desire drives this process (a fact which can be quite disconcerting in the sober eyes of colleagues, aware of the growing adulation shown by the class). This lecturer creates seductive questions rather than provides seductive answers, s/he is not selling a world view where 'packages' of knowledge can be taught, learnt, reproduced and graded. Students are rather asked to reflect and to follow their lecturer in his/her quest for knowledge. Whatever the students produce, there will always be more questions which lead to new analyses and investigations. Thus the teacher will set in motion the desire for knowledge and a creative process where *connaissance* and *savoir* interact.

The Analyst's discourse is a combination of the above in so far that the teacher positions him/herself as subject-supposed-to-know, the specialist who has knowledge which is not easily available to the student (just like the lecturer in the University discourse) or, alternatively, the Other who sees his/her students and expects them to achieve (as in the Hysteric's discourse). This sets the subject's desire in motion, the desire to know what the teacher knows (not what the teacher/lecturer lacks in terms of knowledge), or the desire to achieve as the teacher expects the subject to achieve (Master's discourse).

The lecturer/teacher who has an Analyst's discourse will present him/herself as a kind of 'silent master within the university discourse' in so far that s/he is 'the one who knows' and expects the students to 'produce' knowledge (*savoir* as opposed to *connaissance*) which s/he knows the students 'have'. Further, they are expected to take intellectual risks (in other words, 'just let it happen'). Just as in the Hysteric's discourse, students will feel empowered. Primarily this lecturer is interested in seeing his/her students grow, as opposed to being the object of desire (which is the case in the Hysteric's discourse). As I have written earlier, the analyst/lecturer is often claimed to understand his/her proselytes, calling upon their hidden capacities, demanding that they go beyond themselves. This can be quite a frustrating experience at first, as students do not, at the outset, understand what the lecturer/teacher is aiming at. Not until the students have their first experiences of subject creativity do they start to settle in this rather unusual climate where anything can happen.

The lecture itself can become a creative endeavour for those who are prepared to relinquish control and move away from lesson plans. Lecturers/teachers who allow for subject creativity to emerge during their lessons will create a climate where this will happen more easily for their students (seeing that the lecturer/teacher is a role model). However, this climate is also dependent on students allowing the teacher to relinquish control. Students can either facilitate such a climate or set up barriers, demanding that the teacher keep to a clear lesson plan. Basadur and Hausdorf (1996) describe how organisational attitudes such as having no time for new ideas or valuing new ideas affect creativity in organisations. Therefore, any attempt to develop an environment for creative endeavour is a two-way affair. Time should always be given to arriving at an agreement as to 'what goes', as there are students who can feel very uncomfortable with the lack of control that the development of a creative environment might demand.

The classroom is an ideal environment for creative endeavour. Free association may arise when a student asks the teacher questions concerning his/her personal experience, which in turn often causes the teacher to sift through memories, describing one after another, thus causing the teacher to be thrown out on to an associative trajectory. Even if the teacher's own sense of order brings him/her back to 'reality', similar questions from other students may cause the story teller to emerge again and a whole hour can pass immersed in one of these narratives. The lecturer may attempt to solve problems which emerge in relation to student questions (the subject speaks when the ego is in doubt), seemingly immersed in the argument, almost intractable when considering the content. Students often wish for more interesting stories and the teacher's story teller produces what is expected (man's desire is the desire of the Other). The magnetic quality of the gaze, in other words, can account for the shift in emphasis from free association to expectation. The prompting provided by students' questions is the main difference between creativity observed in dreams and creativity which emerges in the classroom. The strange logic of the dream narrative is allowed to work undisturbed during the night. However, in the classroom questions are posed which set the 'story teller' in motion and direct its activity (just as the therapist's questions direct the analysand's subject during therapy).

Summary

Modern art can be used as a part of creative methodology for individuals 'sensitive' to the visual arts. Many modern artists have created their work with an aim to resist interpretive attempts by the ego. Installations involving electronic material, architectural work and IT can be used to elicit subject creativity in a range of subjects such as maths, physics, chemistry, etc. Free associative techniques can also be used, as can mindfulness or relaxation (both cognitive research and psychoanalytic research support these methods). Double negation, riddles and nonsensical statements are only some of the techniques used by writers to avoid the ego's interpretive attempts. Poetry can both elicit and be produced by *savoir*. The interrelations between teachers and students are instrumental in developing a classroom climate that facilitates creativity, as are attitudes and approaches to creativity within organisations. The lecture can in and of itself be a creative endeavour if *savoir* is allowed to emerge. The lecturer's/teacher's approach to creativity is important as s/he is a role model.

Conclusion

Creativity is inherent to all human beings and is not dependent on IQ or genetic inheritance. While these factors might help to emphasise creative capacity, they are not necessary. It is more a question as to 'what kind' of creativity we wish to elicit. Subject creativity, the material often used by artists, writers and musicians, is seen to produce the 'material' which the ego sets 'into place'. IQ and genetic inheritance might enable packaging and marketing of this material. However, they do not affect the underlying mechanisms of creativity.

For teachers in the classroom, a variety of methods are open for use. These are relatively simple, but they demand courage. Subject creativity is best achieved through a release of control, something many teachers are uncomfortable with and few educational institutions condone. Further, research indicates that 'creativity' is seldom at a high premium in educational institutions, where the Master's discourse is one of the most common. Many of us use this discourse, some of us all the time owing to the culture of educational institutions and the logistics of 'running' a classroom. The Master's discourse emphasises the production of knowledge and excellence, but little credence is given to creative endeavour unless it is part of the curriculum. The same can be said for higher education. Here the University discourse places ever greater emphasis on the production of knowledge as a support for the organisation and the lecturer's *raison d'être*. Only where teachers and lecturers dare to place themselves in the position of 'desire', either as the object or as the faulty divided subject, will creativity be central to the educational process. Some teachers do this some of the time, few teachers do it all of the time.

Research discussed in this book points to pedagogy being an art form. While the Master's and University discourses limit the subject creativity of the students, they do not limit subject creativity emerging during a lecture. This is open to all discourses and, in fact, some teachers/lecturers in the Master's and University discourses are appreciated precisely because they lecture 'out there with the Other'. Wrapped up in their subjects (whatever these might be) and the production of knowledge, they can at times easily and inadvertently be led off on a tangent of free association (which is diffi-cult in the Hysteric's and Analyst's discourses, where the lecturer/teacher is wrapped up in student development). These 'subject' lectures can act to cement the status of the lecturer/teacher in the University and Master's dis-courses. They might even draw great audiences, create a good reputation for the educational establishment where they take place, lead to televised lectures and programmes, etc. The successful 'creative' lecturer can turn their craft into a lucrative business when combined with the Master's or University discourse. Here the audience capacity to interpret the lecturer's work is brought to bear on the contents of the lecture as creative activity (as opposed to productivity). Creativity in different 'forms', then, can be inherent to all discourses.

Repetition and a tendency to 'cling' to old knowledge is not conducive to creativity. However, the great investments made by the ego when acquiring *connaissance* leads to the probability that it (the ego) will defend its hard-earned gains. Bauman points to the importance of 'letting old knowledge go' in postmodern society. Rigid defence of acquired know-ledge is no longer conducive to a 'fluid life'. Repression and neurotic symp-toms also cement 'old memories'. While the mechanisms underlying the neurotic symptom are creative, the insistence of the neurotic symptom is not. Neither are masochistic machinations, blocking creative endeavour with rigid self-criticism or sabotaging their success. The death drive then can be detrimental to creative endeavour.

Creative listening can emerge in relation to the Other when we tuck away our egos and stop trying to create meaning in our meeting with the Other. This is another kind of listening (similar in part to that which emerges during lectures eliciting subject creativity). The Other, then, is central to subject creativity. However, primary narcissism, the foundation of all human relations, can sabotage the emergence of creativity when meetings with the other/Other elicit competitive aggressivity (endemic to the classroom) or, worse, aggression. Further, the structure of educational organisations, where one lecturer works with groups including 30 and upwards students, can elicit feelings of helplessness or a lack of recognition in some students at some times (when students find it difficult to make themselves heard or recognised for their work in their group). This in turn can lead to melancholic affect and unruly behaviour, which are also endemic to the classroom. We can only be aware of the mechanisms behind a sudden outbreak of aggressivity or unruliness and attempt to ameliorate these by avoiding uneven competition, supplying platforms for communi-cation, supporting democratic structures and providing sources of signifiers along which tension can be dissipated (the pleasure principle).

Finally, making room for subject creativity.

The ambient space of the classroom allows for the emergence of beyond. A beyond weaving itself into existence through the dream narrative, meandering its way through symbols, sentence by sentence, page by page, exploding in colour on to the artists canvas, emerging through strange music still playing on the composer's lips when awaking at dawn.

This subject will speak if only we listen, allowing access to a source of creativity inherent to all. We do not need to have the genius of a Dostoevsky, but the courage of one, to allow for that 'moment of madness' when the 'flood gates open'. And Schiller should know, as his burning desire to create kept him alive through many consumptive years where other perished before him.

The subject speaks when called on to do so by the Other, by the gaze of the Other, by the invocation and the desire. The Other commands us from beyond, from within and without the object. Signifiers spill forth from our lips, like poetry disjointed but true, the Other interprets, the other speaks and our egos suddenly see a new meaning. Signifiers fall like droplets and then forge forth in a steady flow, our chapters emerge, evolve and grow, fanning out into so many books, so many thesis. This magic is the steady undercurrent of our minds.

Knowledge is the object of desire, though the master would never know to look at it, more is the measure, forever more, setting the student to work. Where students produce 'true' knowledge they have responded to a riddle, 'I think where I am not', and the oracle smiles without providing the answers. But the Other responds. Desire pulls forth the signifiers when faced with lack of the Other, wishing to heal the gap, not suspecting that s/he already holds the key, is in fact the object and wishes to be discovered as such. 'Go forth and learn more', results only in division, more lack while the university lecturer feeds on the signifiers produced by the students.

There is pleasure also, there is *jouissance* beyond pleasure. The discourses of knowledge are permeated by both. *Jouissance* dances on the side of the master, on the side of the lecturer, while the students gain pleasure from the knowledge amassed, *jouissance* only afforded to those who are called on to cover the lack or to discover the knowledge inherent to the agent, *connaissance* and *savoir* forever mingling and merging, creators of creation and so on.

We are all artists, then, in the field of the Other, caught in the gaze.

Bibliography

Adams, P. (1996) *The Emptiness of the Image: Psychoanalysis and Sexual Differences*. London and New York: Routledge.

Albert, R. S. (1978) Observations and suggestions regarding giftedness, familial influence and the achievement of eminence. *Gifted Child Quarterly* 22, 201–211.

Amabile, T. M. and Gryskiewicz, N. D. (1989) The creative environment scales: Work environment inventory. *Creativity Research Journal* 2, 231–253.

American Psychiatric Association (1994) *Diagnostic and Statistical Manual of Mental Disorders*, 4th edition (DSM-IV). Washington, DC: APA.

Arieti, S. (1976) *Creativity: The Magic Synthesis*. New York: Basic Books.

Aristotle (2001) *The Basic Works of Aristotle*. New York: Random House.

Bachtold, L. M. (1973) Personality characteristics of creative women. *Perceptual and Motor Skills* 36, 311–319.

Bacon, F. (2002) *Francis Bacon: The Major Works including New Atlantis and the Essays*. Oxford: Oxford University Press.

Barron, F. (1963) The need for order and for disorder as motives in creative activity. In C. W. Taylor and F. Barron (eds), *Scientific Creativity: Its Recognition and Development*, 153–160. New York: Wiley.

Basadur, M. and Hausdorf, P. A. (1996) Measuring divergent thinking attitudes related to creative problems solving and innovation management. *Creativity Research Journal* 9, 1, 21–32.

Bauman, Zygmunt (1995) *Life in Fragments: Essays in Postmodern Moralities*. Oxford: Blackwell.

Bergstedt, B. (1998) *Den livsupplysande texten: en läsning av N. F. S. Grundtvigs-pedagogiska skrifter*. Stockholm: Carlsson.

Blixen, K. (1989) *Out of Africa*. London: Cresset Press.

Blixen, K. (2002) *Seven Gothic Tales*. London: Penguin.

Boethius (2002) *The Consolation of Philosophy*. New York: Dover Publications, Inc.

Bowers, K. S., Regehr, G., Balshazard, C. and Parker, K. (1990) Intuition in the context of discovery. *Cognitive Psychology* 22, 72–110.

Brewin, C. (2003) *Post Traumatic Stress Disorder: Malady or Myth?* New Haven and London: Yale University Press.

Carlsson, I. (2002) Anxiety and flexibility of defense related to high or low creativity. *Creativity Research Journal* 14, 341–349.

Carlsson, I., Wendt, P. E. and Risberg, J. (2000) On the neurobiology of creativity:

Differences in frontal activity between high and low creative subjects. *Neuropsychologia* 38, 873–885.

Church, J. (1961) *Language and the Discovery of Reality. A Developmental Psychology of Cognition.* New York: Random House.

Cicero, M. T. (2008), M. T. *On Obligations.* Oxford: Oxford University Press.

Crutchfield, R. S. (1962) Conformity and creative thinking. In H. E. Gruber, G. Terell and M. Wertheimer (eds), *Contemporary Approaches to Creative Thinking: A Symposium Held at the University of Colorado.* New York: Athernon.

Damasio, A. R. (1994) *Descartes' Error: Emotion, Reason, and the Human Brain.* New York: G.P. Putnam.

Damasio, A. R. (1999) *The Feeling of What Happens: Body, Emotion and the Making of Consciousness.* London: Vintage.

Damasio, A. R. (2001) Some notes on brain, imagination and creativity. In K. H. Pfenninger and V. R. Shubik (eds), *The Origins of Creativity*, 59–68. Oxford: Oxford University Press.

Derrida, J. (1972) *Marges de la Philosophie.* Paris: Éditions de Minuit.

Derrida, J. (1978) *Writing and Difference,* Chicago: University of Chicago Press.

Dollinger, S. J., Urban, K. K. and James, T. J. (2004) Creativity and openness: Further validation of two creative product measures. *Creativity Research Journal* 16, 35–48.

Dostoevsky, F. (1992) *Devils.* Oxford: Oxford University Press.

Dostoevsky, F. (1996) *The Idiot.* Ware: Wordsworth Editions.

Dudek, S. Z. and Verreault, R. (1989) The creative thinking and ego functioning of children. *Creativity Research Journal* 2, 64–86.

Ekvall, G. and Ryhammar, L. (1999) The creative climate: Its determinants and effects at a Swedish university. *Creativity Research Journal* 12, 303–310.

Evans, D. (1996) *An Introductory Dictionary of Lacanian Psychoanalysis.* London: Routledge.

Evans, D. (1998) From Kantian ethics to mystical experience: an exploration of jouissance. In Dany Nobus (ed.), *Key Concepts of Lacanian Psychoanalysis*, 1–28. London: Rebus Press.

Eysenck, H. J. (1997) Creativity and personality. In M. A. Runco (ed.), *Creativity Research Handbook.* Cresskill: Hampton Press.

Eysenck, H. J. (2003) Creativity, personality, and the convergent divergent continuum. In M. A. Runco (ed.), *Critical Creative Processes*, 95–114. Cresskill, NJ: Hampton Press.

Feist, G. (1998) A meta-analysis of personality in scientific and artistic creativity. *Personality and Social Psychology Review* 4, 290–304.

Felman, S. (ed.) (1978) *Literature and Psychoanalysis: The Question of Reading Otherwise.* New Haven: Yale University.

Flaherty, A. W. (2005) Frontotemporal and dopaminergic control of idea generation and creative drive. *Journal of Comparative Neurology* 493, 147–153.

Forster, E. M. (1976) *A Passage to India.* Harmondsworth: Penguin.

Foucault, Michel (1977) *Discipline and Punish: The Birth of the Prison,* translated into English by Richard Howard. Harmondsworth: Penguin.

Foucault, Michel (1984) *The Use of Pleasure: The History of Sexuality,* Vol. 2. Harmondsworth: Penguin.

Foulkes, D. (1982) *Children's Dreams: Longitudinal Studies.* New York: Wiley.

Foulkes, D. (1999) *Children's Dreaming and the Development of Consciousness.* Cambridge: Harvard University Press.

Freud, S. (1893) *Some Points for a Comparative Study of Organic and Hysterical Motor Paralysis*, Standard Edition Vol. I, 157–172. London: Hogarth Press.

Freud, S. (1895) *A Project for a Scientific Psychology*, Standard Edition, Vol. I, 281–397. London: Hogarth Press.

Freud, S. (1900) *The Interpretation of Dreams*, Standard Edition, Vols IV–V. London: Hogarth Press.

Freud, S. (1905) *Fragment of an Analysis of a Case of Hysteria*, Standard Edition, Vol. VII, 1–122. London: Hogarth Press.

Freud, S. (1909) *Analysis of Phobia in a Five Year Old Boy*, Standard Edition, Vol. X, 1–122. London: Hogarth Press.

Freud, S. (1911) *Psycho-Analytic Notes on an Autobiographical Account of a Case of Paranoia (Dementia Paranoides)*, Standard Edition, Vol. XII. London: Hogarth Press.

Freud, S. (1915a) *Instincts and their Vicissitudes*, Standard Edition, Vol. XIV, 110–140. London: Hogarth Press.

Freud, S. (1915b) *Repression*, Standard Edition, Vol. XIV, 141–158. London: Hogarth Press.

Freud, S. (1915c) *The Unconscious*, Standard Edition, Vol. XIV, 159–216. London: Hogarth Press.

Freud, S. (1915d) *Thoughts for the Times on War and Death*, Standard Edition, Vol. XIV, 273–303. London: Hogarth Press.

Freud, S. (1916–1917) *Introductory, Lectures on Psycho-Analysis, Lecture XXV*, Standard Edition, Vol. XVI, 392–411. London: Hogarth Press.

Freud, S. (1917) *Mourning and Melancholia*, Standard Edition, Vol. XIV, 237–258. London: Hogarth Press.

Freud, S. (1918) *From the History of an Infantile Neurosis*, Standard Edition, Vol. XVII, 1–123. London: Hogarth Press.

Freud, S. (1920) *Beyond the Pleasure Principle*, Standard Edition, Vol. XVIII, 1–64. London: Hogarth Press.

Freud, S. (1923) *The Ego and the Id*, Standard Edition, Vol. XIX, 1–66. London: Hogarth Press.

Freud, S. (1926) *Inhibitions, Symptoms and Anxiety*, Standard Edition, Vol. XX, 77–175. London: Hogarth Press.

Freud, S. (1930) *Civilisation and its Discontents*, Standard Edition, Vol. XXI, 57–147. London: Hogarth Press.

Freud, S. (1984 [1924]) *The Economic Problem of Masochism*, Standard Edition, Vol. XIX, 157–170. London: Hogarth.

Fromm, E. (1973) *The Anatomy of Human Destructiveness.* London: Penguin Books.

Gahagan, L. (1936) Sex differences in the recall of stereotyped dreams, sleep-talking and sleep walking. *Journal of Genetic Psychology* 48, 227–236.

Gärdenfors, P. (2001) *Hur homo blev Sapiens: Om tankandets evolution.* Enskede TPB.

George, J. M. and Zhou, J. (2001) When openness to experience and consciousness are related to creative behaviour: An interactional approach. *Journal of Applied Psychology* 86, 513–524.

Gick, M. L. and Holyoak, K. J. (1980) Analogical problem solving. *Cognitive Psychology* 12, 306–355.

Gick, M. L. and Lockhart, R. S. (1995) Analogical problem solving. *Cognitive Psychology* 12, 306–355.

Goertzel, V. and Goertzel, M. G. (1962) *Cradles of Eminence.* Boston, MA: Little, Brown.

Goldberg, E., Podell, K. and Lovell, M. (1994) Lateralization of frontal lobe functions and cognitive novelty. *Journal of Clinical and Experimental Neuropsychiatry* 22, 56–68.

Golann, S. E. (1962) The creative motive. *Journal of Personality* 30, 588–600.

Goleman, D. (1995) *Emotional Intelligence.* London: Bloomsbury Publishing Plc.

Griffin, M. and McDermott, M. R. (1998) Exploring a tripart relationship between rebelliousness, openness to experience, and creativity. *Social Behavior and Personality* 26, 347–356.

Griffith, R., Miyago, O. and Tago, A. (1958) The universality of typical dreams: Japanese vs. Americans. *American Anthropologist* 60, 1173–1179.

Gruber, H. E. (1988) The evolving systems approach to creative work. *Creativity Research Journal* 1, 27–51.

Guastello, S., Shissler, J., Driscoll, J. and Hyde, T. (1998) Are some cognitive styles more creatively productive than others? *Creativity Research Journal* 32, 77–91.

Guilford, J. P. (1967) Framing reference for creative behaviour in the arts. In J. C. Gowan *et al.* (eds), *Creativity: Its Educational Implications,* 189–195. New York: John Wiley and Co.

Hagh-Shenas, H., Goldstein, L. and Yule, W. (1999) Psychobiology of post traumatic stress disorder. In W. Yulem (ed.), *Post Traumatic Stress Disorder: Concepts and Therapy,* 139–160. New York: John Wiley and Sons.

Harlow, J. M. (1868) Recovery from the passage of an iron bar through the head. *Publications of the Massachussetts Medical Society* 2, 327–347.

Harman, W. and Rheingold, H. (1984) *Higher Creativity: Liberating the Unconscious for Breakthrough Insights.* New York: Penguin Putnam.

Harrington, D. M. (1981) Creativity, analogical thinking and muscular metaphors. *Journal of Mental Imagery* 6, 121–126.

Hartmann, E. (1984) *The Nightmare: The Psychology and Biology of Terrifying Dreams.* New York: Basic Books.

Hasenfus, N., Martindale, C. and Birnbaum, D. (1983) Psychological reality of cross-media artistic styles. *Journal of Experimental Psychology: Human perception and performance* 9, 841–863.

Hauge, H. (1995) *Den litteraere vending: dekonstruktiv videnskabsteori.* Århus: Modtryck.

Hebb, D. O. (1949) *The Organization of Behavior.* New York: Wiley.

Hegel, G. W. F. (2003) *The Phenomenology of Mind.* New York: Dover Publications, Inc.

Herbert, A. (2006) *Lacan and PTSD with a Special Focus on Victims of Torture.* Lund: Punctum Studier.

Herbert, A. and Bergstedt, B. (2008) *Kunskapen och Språket: om pedagogiken, texten och hjärnan.* Liber: AB.

Heynick, F. (1993) *Language and its Disturbances in Dreams: The Pioneering Work of Freud and Kraeplin Updated.* New York: Wiley.

Hobson, J. A., Pace-Schott, E. and Stickgold, R. (2000) Dreaming and the brain: Towards a cognitive neuroscience of conscious states. *Behavioral and Brain Sciences*, 23, 6, 793–842.

Hofstadter, D. (1985) *Metamagical Themas: Questing for the Essence of Mind and Patterns.* New York: Bantam Books.

Hyldgaard, K. (2008) *Videnskapsteori: en grundbog til de pedagogiske fag.* Fredriksberg: Roskilde Universitetsforlag.

James, W. (1880) Great men, great thoughts, and the environment (lecture delivered before the Harvard Natural History Society). *Atlantic Monthly,* October. Reproduced at www.emory.edu/EDUCATION/mfp/jgreatmen.html.

Jung, C. G. (1962) *Psychological Types.* New York: Pantheon.

Kant, I. (2000) *The Critique of Pure Reason.* Guernsey: Guernsey Press Co. Ltd.

Kaun, D. E. (1991) Writers die young: The impact of work and leisure on longevity. *Journal of Economic Psychology* 12, 381–399.

Keller, H. (1909) *Min Värld*, Stockholm: Hugo Gebers förlag.

Koestler, A. (1964) *The Act of Creation.* New York: MacMillan.

Kojève, A. (1969) *Introduction to the Reading of Hegel.* New York: Basic Books, Inc.

Kolb, B. and Whishaw, I. Q. (1999) *Fundamentals of Human Neuropsychology.* New York: Worth Publishers.

Kramer, M. D. (2007) *The Dream Experience: A Systematic Exploration.* New York and London: Routledge.

Kris, E. (1952) *Psychoanalytic Explorations in Art.* New York: International Universities Press.

Kristeva, J. (1991) *Strangers to Ourselves*, trans. L. S. Roudiez. New York: Columbia University Press.

Lacan, J. (1953–1954) *Freud's Papers on Technique: The Seminar of Jacques Lacan, Book I*, edited by Jacques-Alain Miller, trans. with notes John Forrester: New York and London: W. W. Norton & Company.

Lacan, J. (1954–1955) *The Ego in Freud's Theories and in the Technique of Psychoanalysis: The Seminar of Jacques Lacan, Book II*, edited by Jacques-Alain Miller, trans. Sylvia Tomaselli, notes John Forrester. New York and London: W. W. Norton & Company.

Lacan, J. (1955–1956) *The Psychoses: The Seminar of Jacques Lacan, Book III*, edited by Jacques-Alain Miller, trans. with notes by Russel Grigg. London: Routledge.

Lacan, J. (1956–1957) *Le Seminaire: Livre IV, La relation d'objet.* Paris: Champ Freudien.

Lacan, J. (1959–1960) *The Ethics of Psychoanalysis: The Seminars of Jacques Lacan, Book VII*, edited by Jacques-Alain Miller, trans. with notes by Dennis Porter. London: Routledge.

Lacan, J. (1962–1963) *Anxiety (Seminar X)*, unpublished notes.

Lacan, J. (1964) *The Four Fundamental Concepts of Psychoanalysis*, edited by Jacques-Alain Miller, trans. Alan Sheridan, Introduction by David Macey. London: Vintage.

Lacan, J. (1966) *Ecrits: A Selection*, trans. A. Sheridan. London: Tavistock Publications.

Lacan, J. (1969–1970) *The Other Side of Psychoanalysis: The Seminar of Jacques Lacan Book XVII*, trans. Russell Grigg. New York: W.W. Norton.

Lacan, J. (1972–1973) *On Feminine Sexuality, The Limits of Love and Knowledge, Encore: The Seminar of Jacques Lacan, Book XX*, edited by Jacques-Alain Miller, trans. with notes Bruce Fink. New York and London: W. W. Norton and Company.

Lacan, J. (1974–1975) 'Le Séminaire XII', R.S.I. *Ornicar?* Vol. 2–5.

Laplanche, J. and Pontalis, J. B. (1988) *The Language of Psychoanalysis*. London: Karnac Books.

Le Doux, J. E. (1998) *The Emotional Brain*. London: Weidenfeld and Nicolson.

Lenz Taguchi, H. (2000) *Emancipation och motstånd: dokumentation och kooperativa läroprocesser i förskolan*. Stockholm: HLS förlag.

Levinas, E. (1969) *Totality and Infinity: An Essay on Exteriority*. Pittsburgh: Duquesne University Press.

Lévi-Strauss, C. (1958) *Anthropologie structurale*. Paris: Plon.

Lévi-Strauss, C. (1962) *La pensée sauvage*. Paris: Plon.

Luria, A. R. (1968) *The Mind of a Mnemonist*. New York: Basic Books.

Luria, A. R. (1976) *Cognitive Development: Its Cultural and Social Foundations*. Cambridge, MA: Harvard University Press.

McCrae, R. R. (1987) Creativity, divergent thinking, and openness to experience. *Journal of Personality and Social Psychology* 52, 1258–1265.

Martindale, C. (1988) Aesthetics, psychobiology and cognition. In F. H. Farley and R. Neperud (eds), *The Foundations of Aesthetics in Art Education*. New York: Plenum.

Martindale, C. (1998) Aesthetics, psychobiology and cognition. In F. H. Farley and R. Neperud (eds), *The Foundation of Aesthetics in Art and Art Education*. New York: Plenum.

Martindale, C. (1999) The biological basis of creativity. In R. J. Sternberg (ed.), *Handbook of Creativity*, 137–152. Cambridge: Cambridge University Press.

Martindale, C. and Hasenfus, N. (1978) EEG differences as a function of the creative process, and effort to be original. *Biological Psychology* 3, 6, 157–167.

Martindale, C., Covello, E. and West, A. (1986) Primary processes and hemispheric asymmetry. *Journal of Genetic Psychology* 147, 79–87.

Mednick, S. A. (1962) The associative basis for the creative process. *Psychological Review* 69, 220–232.

Miller, A. (1996) Metaphors in creative scientific thought. *Creativity Research Journal* 9, 113–122.

Miller, J. A. (1996) Commentary on Lacan's Text, trans. Bruce Fink. In Richard Felstein, Bruce Fink and Maire Jaanus (eds) *Reading Seminars I and II: Lacan's Return to Freud*, 212–237. Albany: State University of New York Press.

Miller, J. A. (2001) The symptom and the body event, edited by A. Badiou and S. Zizek. *Lacanian Ink* 19.

Molle, M., Marshall, L., Lutzenberger, W., Pietrowsky, R., Fehm, H. L. and Born, J. (1996) Enhanced dynamic complexity in the human EEG during creative thinking. *Neuroscience Letters* 208, 61–64.

Molle, M., Marshall, L., Wolf, B., Fehm, H. L. and Born, J. (1999) EEG complexity and performance measures of creative thinking. *Psychophysiology* 36, 95–104.

Nietzche, F. (2000) *Basic Writings of Nietzsche*. New York: Random House.

Nobus, D. (1998) Life and death in the glass: a new look at the mirror stage. In D. Nobus (ed.), *Key Concepts of Lacanian Psychoanalysis*, 101–138. London: Rebus Press.

Nobus, D. (2000) *Jacques Lacan and the Freudian Practice of Psychoanalysis*. London and Philadelphia: Routledge.

Nopple, L. D. (1996) Progression in the service of the ego, cognitive styles, and creative thinking. *Creativity Research Journal* 9, 369–383.

Noy, P. (1969) A revision of the psychoanalytic theory of the primary processes. *International Journal of Psychoanalysis* 50, 2, 155–178.

Okuda, S. M., Runco, M. A. and Berger, D. E. (1991). Creativity and the finding and solving of real-world problems. *Journal of Psycho-educational Assessment* 9, 117–129.

Parnes, S. J. (1967) *Creative Behavior Guidebook*. New York: Scribners.

Petrides, M. and Milner, B. (1982) Deficits on subject ordered tasks after frontal- and temporal-lobe lesions in man. *Neuropsychologia* 20, 249–262.

Petsche, H. (1996) Approaches to verbal, visual and musical creativity by EEG coherence analysis. *International Journal of Psycho-physiology* 24, 145–159.

Plato (1997) *Plato: Complete Works*. Indianapolis: Hackett Publishing Company.

Prahbu, V., Sutton, C. and Sauser, W. (2008) Creativity and certain personality traits: Understanding the mediating effect of intrinsic motivation. *Creativity Research Journal* 20, 1, 53–66.

Ramachandran, V. S. and Hirstein, W. (1999). The science of art: A neurological theory of aesthetic experience. *Journal of Consciousness Studies* 6, 15–31.

Rauch, S. L. *et al.* (1996) A symptom provocation study of post traumatic stress disorder using positron emission tomography and script-driven imagery. *Archives of General Psychiatry* 53, 380–387.

Rimbaud, A. (2005) *Complete Works, Selected Letters: A Bilingual Edition*. Chicago: University of Chicago Press.

Root-Bernstein, R. S. (1989) *Discovering: Inventing and Solving Problems at the Frontier of Scientific Research*. Cambridge, MA: Harvard University.

Rothenberg, A. (1990) Creativity, mental health and alcoholism. *Creativity Research Journal* 3, 179–201.

Rothenberg, A. (1999) Janusian processes. In M. A. Runco and S. R. Pritzker (eds), *Encyclopedia of Creativity*, 103–108. San Diago: Academic Press.

Roudinesco, E. (1997) *Jacques Lacan & Co: A History of Psychoanalysis in France, 1925–1985*, trans. Jeffrey Mehlman. London: Free Association Books.

Runco, M. A. (1985) Reliability and convergent validity of ideational flexibility as a function of academic achievement. *Perceptual and Motor Skills* 61, 1075–1081.

Runco, M. A. (1999) Contrarianism. In M. A. Runco and S. R. Pritzker (eds), *Encyclopedia of Creativity*, Vol 1, 367–371. London: Academic Press.

Runco, M. A. (2006) Reasoning and personal creativity. In J. C. Kaufman and J. Baer (eds), *Creativity and Reason in Cognitive Development*. Cambridge: Cambridge University Press.

Runco, M. A. (2007) *Creativity: Theories and Themes: Research, Development and Practice*. Amsterdam: Elsevier.

Runco, M. A. and Chand, I. (1995) Cognition and creativity. *Educational Psychology Review* 7, 243–267.

Runco, M. A, Johnson, D., Baer, P. (1993) Parents' and teachers' implicit theories of children's creativity. *Child Study Journal* 23, 91–113.

Sachs, O. (1989) *Seeing Voices: A Journey into the World of the Deaf.* Berkeley: University of California Press.

Scott, M. E. (1985) How stress can affect gifted/creative potential: Ideas to better insure realization of potential. *Creative Child and Adult Quarterly* 10, 240–249.

Shakespeare, W. (1994a) *Macbeth.* London: Penguin.

Shakespeare, W. (1994b) *Hamlet.* London: Penguin.

Smith, G. J. W. and Amner, G. (1997) Creativity and perception. In M. A. Runco (ed.) *Creativity Research Handbook*, Vol. 1, 67–82. Cresskill: Hampton Press.

Smith, S. M. and Dodds, R. A. (1999) Incubation. In M. A. Runco and S. R. Pritzker (eds) *Encyclopedia of Creativity*, 39. San Diago: Academic Press.

Snyder, F. (1970) The phenomenology of dreaming. In L. Meadow and L. Stone (eds), *The Psychodynamic Implications of the Physiological Studies of Dreams*, 124–151. Springfield: C.C. Thomas.

Solms, M. (1997) *The Neuropsychology of Dreams: A Clinico-Anatomical Study.* Mahwah, NJ: Lawrence Erlbaum.

Solms, M. and Turnbull, O. (2005) *Hjärnan och den inre världen: en introduktion till psykoanalysens neurovetenskapliga grunder*, Stockholm: Natur och kultur.

Sperry, R. (1964) The great cerebral commissure. *Scientific American* 210, 1, 42–52.

Squire, L. R. and Kandel, E. R. (1999) *Memory: From Mind to Molecules.* New York: Scientific American Library.

Sternberg, R. J. and Lubart, T. I. (1996) Investing in creativity. *American Psychologist* 51, 7, 77–88.

Sulloway, F. (1996) *Born to Rebel.* New York: Pantheon.

Taft, R. (1971) Creativity: Hot and cold. *Journal of Personality* 39, 345–361.

Tegano, D. W. (1990) Relationship of tolerance of ambiguity and playfulness to creativity. *Psychological Reports* 66, 1047–1056.

Thomas, N. G. and Berk, L. E. (1981) Effects of school environments on the development of young children's creativity. *Child Development* 52, 1153–1162.

Todd, S. (1997) *Learning Desire: Perspectives on Pedagogy, Culture, and the Unsaid.* New York: Routledge.

Todd, S. (2003) *Learning from the Other: Levinas, Psychoanalysis, and Ethical Possibilities in Education.* Albany: State University of New York Press.

Torrance, E. P. (1962) *Guiding Creative Talent.* Englewood Cliffs: Prentice-Hall.

Torrance, E. P. (1963) The creative personality and the ideal pupil. *Teachers College Record* 65, 220–226.

Torrance, E. P. (1972) Can we teach children to think creativity? *The Journal of Creative Behavior* 6, 114–141.

Torrance, E. P. (1995) *Why Fly?*. Norwood, NJ: Ablex.

Vetlesen, A. J. (1994) *Perception, Empathy and Judgement: An Inquiry into the Preconditions of Moral Performance.* University Park: Pennsylvania State University Press.

Wallach, M. A. and Kogan, N. (1965) *Modes of Thinking in Young Children.* New York: Holt, Rinehart & Winston.

Wallas, G. (1926) *The Art of Thought*. New York: Harcourt Brace and World.

Westby, E. L. and Dawson, V. L. (1995) Creativity: Asset or burden in the classroom? *Creativity Research Journal* 8, 1–10.

Wild, C. (1965) Creativity and adaptive regression. *Journal of Personality and Social Psychology* 2, 161–169.

Winson, J. (1990) The meaning of dreams. *Scientific American* 263, 5, 86–8, 90–2, 94–6.

Woolf, V. (2000) *The Waves*. London: Wordsworth Editions.

Zangwill, O. L. (1966) Psychological deficits associated with frontal lobe lesions. *International Journal of Neurology* 5, 395–402.

Žižek, S. (1998) The seven veils of fantasy. In D. Nobus (ed.), *Key Concepts of Lacanian Psychoanalysis*. London: Rebus Press.

Žižek, S. (2000) *The Fragile Absolute – Or Why is the Christian Legacy Worth Fighting For?* London: Verso.

Index